THE DARK GODDESS

Awakens

An Encoded Transmission to Activate
Original Divine Feminine Blueprints

by

NICOLE MENDOZA

With Channeled Activation Sigils by Daria Robinson

PRAISE FOR NICOLE MENDOZA

"In her book, *The Dark Goddess Awakens*, Nicole takes readers on a mystical and transformational journey within. As she shares the blueprint of her own evolution through trauma healing, Nicole graciously translates the lessons and inspiration that guided her way. Readers will embark on a voyage to explore the wonders of their soul, and to awaken the limitless power that lives within us all."

– Iman Gatti

Author of *Cracked Open – Never Broken*

"Nicole Mendoza makes a deep topic like dark feminine power normal, relatable, and accessible. A guidebook for everyone with a feminine spirit who is ready to embrace themselves as whole beings and step into their full power."

– Teresa Cruz Foley

founder of Brave Space Consulting

DISCLAIMER

The author does not intend this book as a replacement for professional medical advice from a physician or licensed mental health specialist. The reader should regularly consult with such an expert in matters regarding their health, particularly if any symptoms suggest the need for diagnosis or treatment.

The content of this book is intended to provide general information only. While all efforts are made to keep it accurate and current, no warranties, either expressed or implied, are given about the completeness, accuracy, reliability, suitability, or availability with respect to the information, products, services, or related graphics contained in this book for any purpose. Any use of this information is undertaken at one's own risk.

The material within this book is for spiritual and educational purposes only, and its application is the reader's sole responsibility.

DEDICATION

To all the versions of me, from this life and past ones, I offer up this book in gratitude. Every step I have taken, every lesson I have learned, and every experience I have endured has given me the strength and wisdom to accept this reincarnation of myself and has contributed to the woman I have become and who I have yet to be. You have given me the strength to transmute pain into resilience, grief into growth, and suffering into courage. This book is a tribute to our shared journey of self-discovery and transformation. May this book serve as a reminder that we are on an infinite quest for self-discovery and evolution. Here's to us.

But while the sun may be shining brightly, all is not always at peace.

For us, this infinite potential and power remain untapped, hidden away in the depths of our souls like an unopened gift.

We are unable to find courage in our true essence and unsure how to access it even if it did happen to appear.

We are fragmented and broken, unsure if or how we can ever reclaim the original essence we've lost.

The stars that should be shining down from the boundless sky remain dim and distant, out of reach.

We don't know where to turn or where to look; for whom do we call for answers? How can we bridge the gap between what is and what could be?

The brilliance of our divine femininity lies forgotten in the dust as we battle against a reality filled with obstacles and challenges that seem insurmountable.

We are no longer beings with infinite potential and power; instead, we are mere humans searching desperately for something to hold onto.

CONTENTS

Preface

ANSWERING THE CALL OF THE DIVINE ORDER OF THE DARK FEMININE

"You can't run away from yourself."

-Bob Marley

September 2020 marked a turning point in my life, where the unexpected twists of fate thrust me into the realm of dark feminine energy, forever altering the course of my journey. In the middle of a global pandemic that left me unemployed, my world was upended in a mere day. Though I had been slowly progressing in an herbalism apprenticeship that excited me, I felt like I was starting from scratch again—no job, freshly divorced, and a single mother caring for a toddler with emerging developmental delays.

Amidst my anxiousness and sorrow, I found a glimmer of hope. My uncle had just offered me the chance to stay rent-free in the house I had been renting from him, provided I completed some minor maintenance tasks. It was a respite from my grief of the death of my old life and something which gave me a newfound purpose. I finally had the opportunity to gain some stability. Every penny of my student loan checks, the only worthwhile bounty from the pursuit of a now seemingly worthless doctoral degree, was devoted to creating a safe haven for my autistic son and restoring our broken home after the departure of his father.

I remember going to bed one night feeling at peace, and waking up the following day to my uncle's sudden demand for market-rate rent, complete with a two-week notice to vacate his premises if I couldn't find $2,000 a month to pay him. The heartache and betrayal were overwhelming, yet within me arose a flicker of hope that urged me forward.

I tried reaching out to any "family" I had for help. I was met with nothing but, "No." This wasn't the first time I had foolishly called upon them, hoping they'd find it in their hearts to offer me some care or assistance, only to be hurt and disappointed when they didn't show the slightest empathy or compassion.

Amidst the icy winds of uncertainty, a voice within me spoke sternly, "Don't you dare beg for *anything*." At that moment, something shifted within me. I had endured enough of pleading for love, support, and validation, whether in a failed marriage or seeking familial assistance. It was time to acknowledge my worth, honor my boundaries, and hold my head high. With dignity intact, I packed my bags, ready to face whatever lay ahead.

I was in the throes of my most significant spiritual awakening yet. Around the time I started my work with herbs and plant spirits, I began to hear voices and songs in my head that sounded like otherworldly languages. At that time, I also started to connect more frequently with my Higher self and began consciously seeking guidance and communication from my guides, angels, ancestors, and galactic beings. The more I connected, the more the urge to speak these strange languages intensified. I started seeing videos on TikTok and YouTube about "light language," a channeled modality for energy healing and communicating messages. I felt instantly called to begin not only speaking these channeled frequencies, but to also record myself doing so, so that I could publicly post the transmissions and healings. If you have ever seen someone channeling light language, it is about as far out in the realm of "woo" as you can get. A good amount of these messages communicate information about aliens and galactic histories and are from all kinds of "mythical" beings such as fairies and mermaids. For someone like me—desperate to be liked, loved, and accepted—the idea of filming myself speaking these unintelligible sounds, waving my arms around like a mad person, claiming that I had healing from the Pleiadians, dragons, or Ascended Masters seemed insane. But intuitively, I knew channeling light language was essential to whatever changes I hoped would unfold in my life. So despite the discomfort and embarrassment, I kept going.

False friends and an encounter with a catalyst twin flame pushed me to my lowest point in fall 2021. I had gone through all of my savings, liquidated every investment, and was now in a full-blown burnout from pushing myself to start a business making herbal products while still trying to freelance contracts, take care of an autistic toddler, and come to grips with my own fresh autism diagnosis. There was no more money I could borrow. I had no friends or family to call on for support. For the second time in less than a year, I faced the prospect of living in my car with a toddler and possibly on the streets since that would soon be repossessed. The experience with a man I thought was supposed to be my divine counterpart left me energetically dazed and drained. Every day I felt as if I had been run over by a bus, barely able to make it out of bed. And so began my two-year initiation into my path as a High Priestess of the Dark Feminine, and the leg of my soul mission to assist with reclamation and integration of the fragmented soul aspects of the Great Mother.

It was during this dark night of the soul that I found myself drawn even more to channeling light language and connecting with the spiritual realms. My work was gaining a growing following on TikTok (@truenorthawakening), and the interactions from followers kept me diving deeper and deeper into the esoteric. Looking back, perhaps it was just a way to escape the overwhelm and exhaustion of my daily life while still earning a little bit of cash for food and necessities. Regardless, the more I channeled, the more I began to dig into myself as this spiritual being. Certain goddesses started to appear more frequently. They called themselves the Divine Order of the Dark Feminine Collective, and their presence reassured me as they began to guide me through the shadows, anchoring me as I navigated the depths of my psyche.

I had never considered the meaning of femininity, light or dark, until this collective appeared. As the dark feminine goddesses surrounded me and initiated my understanding of this defamed energy, I realized how so many of my destructive ideas and beliefs resulted from the suppression and wounding of my femininity. I had spent decades trying to fit into a box that was far too small for me and any other woman. I had to cut away parts of myself—my wants, needs, preferences, worthiness, and respect—just to appease others. When I reflected upon all I had done to be accepted, I had to sit with the painful realization that nothing had ever seemed to work. No matter how hard I tried, I felt like I had no genuine relationships or meaningful successes. Even when I was married with friends and a professional career, I was still so miserable. An unending ache of anxiety sat heavily on my chest, and I was always terrified something would fall apart if I spoke up. So I did my best to relax when the Dark Feminine Collective beckoned me, vowing to release all the struggle and fighting from within myself and life, simply allowing everything to unfold.

My intuition called me to something greater, but the pain wasn't easing. I welcomed the goddesses who visited more and more often, yet their presence made walking through the underworld an arduous, soul-crushing experience. I'd been praying for a transformative change to heal my waning body and find true love, meaningful connections, stability, and abundance. The Dark Feminine Collective said, "Bet! We've got you." Little did I know that meant moment after moment of every single part of my life tearing apart at the seams.

Kali led the charge, ripping away the old and inauthentic aspects of my life that didn't align with the freedom, love, and abundance I claimed I wanted. Sekhmet was my cheerleader, giving me the courage to continue whenever I felt I would give up. While Inanna consistently held up the mirror of truth, forcing me to really see who I was and challenging me to be comfortable in my own skin, Freya would be there right behind her, helping me to see the value in the parts of myself I'd been ashamed to acknowledge and share. With Hecate's guidance, I set clear boundaries, and Lilith empowered me to vocalize my needs without fear of judgment. Along with a few others, slowly I began to allow myself to bleed. To let out the festering ooze of lifetimes of trauma, painful memories, and stifled emotions that had kept me stagnant. Trust and believe it hurt like hell, but the whole time Mother Tiamat was there, holding me in her womb as I restored my lost pieces, forever showing me glimpses of all the paths I could create with my clear intentions and aligned choices.

Don't get me wrong, my journey has been anything but a smooth, straight road. I have been challenged and tested at each step, facing what has seemed like never-ending loops where I've had to grapple with the different versions of the same people, beliefs, and patterns. I've had to confront parts of myself that I was desperate to bury forever. I remember when my son and I were houseless, on an extended "road trip" across the country, bouncing from motels and couch surfing in between stints in a car that my mom had reluctantly let me borrow before kicking us out. I'd often find myself in some random parking lot, trying to rest without drawing attention or getting into trouble. How could I have gone from achieving a doctorate and having a successful career to being a struggling, single parent sleeping in a car? I had followed all the preset instructions for life to a tee, and even within the spiritual path, I was doing the shadow work, reading the books, and taking all the courses. A million times, I've cried out in soul anguish for any spirit who might listen: "Why me? When will this end?"

I was desperate for any answers or glimmers of hope, and repeatedly devastated at the silence that continued to remind me that no being could answer those questions except me. The torment would not end until I finally allowed myself to be completely honest about who I am, what I desire for my life, and what was in my capacity and true nature to achieve. That was when the real healing work began. And that is when things started to change for the better.

Every tower moment I have endured, and every breakdown I have survived, has been a testament to the resilience and power of dark feminine energy. It ignited a profound change, inspiring me to heal, recognize my desires, and make sure all my choices were true to myself. This is the secret that has been kept from us for so long. No matter how hard we try to meet this concept of divine femininity characterized only by love and light, we will remain fragmented and incomplete, disconnected from our fully complex original essence. All the progress we experience on our spiritual path won't help if we simply try to fit our new understanding into outdated concepts that aim to restrict, silence, and prevent us from being strong and powerful.

In this book, I want to share my story of awakening and self-discovery with you and encourage you to begin your self-initiation to the Divine Order of the Dark Feminine Collective, walking the path of dark feminine reclamation and divine feminine restoration. It is a testimony to the courage and beauty within us all. As you explore the dark feminine energy within, you will find new ways to unlock your potential and reclaim your original state of wholeness. So let us honor the dark feminine energy inside of us, for it holds the keys to discovering our fullest potential and reviving the original divine feminine blueprint. And this, my dear initiate, is the key to restoring balance and harmony not just in yourself but for the entire collective.

INTRODUCTION TO DARK FEMININE ENERGY

"The denial of darkness never equates the abundance of light. And the denial of your actual character never equates to the reality of your best character. ... The caterpillar does not become a butterfly by telling everybody it has wings. It actually buries itself in darkness and grows those wings."

– C. JoyBell C.

You are cordially invited on a grand odyssey of self-discovery and metamorphosis to break the chains of expectation and liberate your soul. *The Dark Goddess Awakens: An Encoded Transmission to Activate Original Divine Feminine Blueprints* will facilitate the unlocking of the power of your dark feminine energy—an inward journey that takes you on a rollercoaster of emotion as you confront the struggles that arise from the repression of feminine archetypes and restore divine balance within yourself. If you have found yourself here, it is no coincidence—your soul is calling out for its freedom. The time is now, this is the journey for you.

This spiritual voyage is designed to unearth and liberate your true self from societal constraints. In these pages, eight powerful dark feminine goddesses will guide you on your path of inner transformation, helping you reconnect with your authentic nature and make decisions that embrace your true essence. Regain stolen power and make the leap into full expression: it's time to begin anew and unshackle yourself.

Before committing to my spiritual path a few years ago, I was stuck in a perpetual cycle of constantly feeling like I didn't quite fit in. It wasn't until I discovered the power of the dark feminine that everything changed. When I did, I stopped running from myself and began exploring my true nature, reclaiming the wild, bold, unapologetic parts of me that I'd been so desperate to hide all those years.

In this book, I hope to empower you to discover who you really are underneath everything everyone's told you that you are or expected you to be, liberating you from societal conditioning. Here you'll harness the transformative power of the dark feminine energy within, unleashing your innate strength and beauty to ignite a world of limitless possibilities.

What is Dark Feminine Energy?

You might be uncertain about accessing any "dark" power, whether it is feminine or not. Believe me, I understand. In spiritual circles, there has been a lot of talk surrounding the ideas of "darkness" and "light." These concepts aren't anything new; people have argued over what they mean and how they affect our lives since the beginning of time.

Let's take a step back and look at the meaning of light and dark. Our society likes to put so-called positive characteristics into the "light" category—love, peace, joy, and so on. Then comes the "dark" side of things, where we place fear, pain, and despair. Here's the thing—these definitions are too limiting! Viewing these concepts in a binary way prevents us from engaging with a more expansive perspective of our world.

Just as a rainbow wouldn't be visible without the rain, we need darkness in our lives to appreciate the light that shines within us. There are so many beautiful ways femininity can be expressed beyond the limited roles society suggests. The dark feminine is bursting with a mysterious power that gives access to intuition, wisdom, and creativity, allowing for kind sensitivity and strong boundaries. Accessing this energy allows you to flow gracefully through life's ups and downs while also transforming tough emotions into art. We're not just here to nurture, be soft, remain still, and love endlessly. There's so much more to it than that!

THE ORIGINS OF THE DARK FEMININE

The Divine Feminine was once an unbroken, radiant force. You might know her by many names, depending on your cultural lens or the slice of time you're peering through: Asherah, Gaia, Yemaya, Pachamama, Tiamat—the list goes on. Picture her as the archetype of all divine femininity and creation. But something happened as consciousness cascaded down through dimensional planes: she splintered. This original Divine Feminine blueprint broke apart like light scattering from a prism, becoming myriad fractals, or splintered versions, of her former self. Over time, these fractals perverted into more unbalanced expressions. The masculine elements of duality nudged this fragmentation along, spiraling her down into denser energies that now manifest as shadowy realms—think Hells, or even Satanic figures. Like shards of a shattered mirror, these fractals have strayed far from their origin, some losing sight of their infinite potential. They're all parts of her, and to make her whole again, they need to be reassembled and healed.

The myths of dark feminine energy can be traced back through centuries, often depicting goddesses using their dark qualities to aid in overcoming difficult situations for both themselves and in the service of others. Rage, destruction, and challenging injustice are just a few ways dark feminine energy has been used to restore balance for not only herself, but for the entire collective. However, while trapped in a fear matrix, society has too often branded certain qualities and emotions as "negative" or "inappropriate," only for them to be twice as frowned upon if a woman expresses them.

Living authentically as a woman can be difficult in contemporary Western culture. We are often trained to bury and ignore these "darker" aspects of femininity and expected to thrive in a heteronormative, patriarchal environment where our genuine expressions of the full range of femininity are met with judgment and condemnation. It's all too common for women to feel like they don't have the freedom to express their anger, grief, or even sometimes joy and desire. This creates issues far too common among feminine-identifying energies, such as shame, people-pleasing tendencies, low self-confidence, and even a lack of self-trust. You further fragment the original blueprint of all that femininity can be when you repress your confidence and autonomy. Having the courage to embrace those aspects is key in helping you become aligned, access your spiritual gifts, and express your highest soul self. Awakening your dark divine feminine energy is a way to honor your emotions and limits, while reclaiming the power that you have been giving away freely for far too long, restoring the original balance of divine femininity within.

The journey back to the original, luminous state of the Divine Feminine Blueprint starts with something so basic yet profound: acceptance and healing. These are the roots of our original essence, the seeds from which we can regrow. As we embark on this cosmic quest to reintegrate the splintered consciousness of the Divine Feminine, we're not just patching up fragments—we're resurrecting the original blueprint to her full glory. And that, my friends, is an endeavor as monumental as it is deeply spiritual.

HOW TO READ THIS BOOK

In this book, the activation of the dormant dark feminine blueprint aspects within you is guided by the story of Tiamat, the primordial goddess of creation. Tiamat was a planetary body in another timeline of Earth's existence, who was destroyed from the collision with another planetary body, Marduk. The explosion caused her matter to be dispersed throughout space/ time dimensions of the cosmos, creating many aspects of our solar system, such as the moon, planets, and aspects of Earth. This myth was known to the ancient Mesopotamians who told an allegory of the story, fashioning Tiamat as the goddess of primordial waters, who had birthed the gods. But as time went by, civilizations and their myths disappeared, and male dominance reigned over creation. The power and true nature of Tiamat was forgotten or maliciously distorted. She was reconceived as a cruel and monstrous figure—a dragon spewing out chaotic monsters to wreak destruction upon everything in its wake, a heartbreaking representation of the crumbling of the divine feminine.

Tiamat possessed a divine power within her being, encompassing the whole blueprint of femininity in its most sublime form—soft and nurturing, yet also exhibiting the strength to shield and protect, mysterious with potent magic and force that could not be fully comprehended. Through her and the other divine energies that have sprung from her, we can remember our true selves and reclaim the forgotten aspects of femininity that have been labeled as "dark." Restoring the energetic body of Tiamat symbolizes reclaiming the powerful and mystical parts of femininity which have been lost, dismissed, or demonized.

The main chapters in this book tap into eight dark goddess energies that hold activation codes for suppressed dark feminine energy. As you read through each one, you will gain insight into Tiamat's story while uncovering how divine feminine energy has been deactivated. I'll share my own journey of awakening and restoring forgotten parts of myself through each goddess's guidance and connection. The goddesses themselves offer unique perspectives and tales through a channeled message. As you get to know them, they'll invite you to embrace their guidance to restore balance to your own life. Finally, it's time for your adventure. You can awaken your dormant dark feminine energy and restore suppressed aspects of your original blueprint with the Original Blueprint Activation Journeys.

ABOUT THE ORIGINAL BLUEPRINT
ACTIVATION JOURNEYS

In this book, the Original Blueprint Activation Journeys (OBAJ) are presented at the end of each chapter. These journeys are channeled invocations, energetically encoded to trigger the codes of the original divine feminine blueprint within you. Each one is written in the first person, so that when you read them—alone, or with others on their dark feminine reclamation journey—your intentions become reality. By speaking these words aloud, coupled with your clear intentions, you awaken your inner creator and further integrate the dark feminine energy, bringing your divine feminine nature back to its original wholeness.

Each OBAJ is unique, and I encourage you to be honest with yourself as you sense the energies of each individual goddess. The journeys were designed to be completed in order, but by all means, follow your heart if an energy or theme calls out to you more powerfully than all the others. You don't need rituals or ceremonies if you don't feel called to do those—let your intuition guide and direct you on your journey. Take your time with it, rereading passages again and again until they really sink in. There's no wrong way to do this.

As you start to work with each goddess, the OBAJ are designed to trigger both conscious and subconscious exploration of the darker parts of yourself. Here, you will face the wounds, limiting beliefs, and hidden shadows holding you back from living your most divine and powerful feminine life. To my fellow trauma survivors—reading this book and doing the journeys could be triggering for you, bringing up powerful emotions. That's okay.

However, if it feels too overwhelming, consider talking to a counselor or therapist as you work through it all. You don't have to go through it alone, and there's no shame in needing help. Deep healing can bring up powerful feelings, even if they've been kept hidden for years. Weigh the options, and give yourself permission to reach out when the time is right.

If you are feeling called, here are a few suggestions that you might find helpful as ways to make the OBAJ sacred and amplify the goddess energy:

- Connect and ground with an element or natural world representation of the goddess energy before and after the activation journey. For example, Inanna is associated with the element of air. Before the OBAJ, you could stand outside and bask in the morning breeze or do some breathwork exercises.

- Use a candle or burn incense to assist in the shift of consciousness. Scent is strongly associated with emotions, memories, and even physiological responses. Take some time to investigate preferred aromas for the goddess energy you are working with, and consider boosting the atmosphere for your journey with an intoxicating odor.

- Create a sacred space in your home where you will engage in the activation journeys. You could create an altar, add comfy pillows and blankets, or adorn it with objects that would help you connect more deeply with the dark feminine energy.

You will see a symbol at the beginning of each of the goddess's chapters, as well as before their respective OBAJ. These are channeled sigils, also known as light codes, that embody the goddess's essence and transmit additional data related to the soul aspect they are activating. It is recommended that you spend two to three minutes gazing softly at the light code, and focus your intention on embodying that soul aspect before beginning work with the goddess, and again before completing the OBAJ.

Working with Deity Energy: A Word on Culture

We are all born with an ancient cosmic code in our DNA, and sometimes we feel called to connect deeply with certain divine beings. Every part of us contains our soul's past lives; in them, we may have incarnated from many parts of the world. You may be called to work with energies from cultures and traditions that are very different from the one you are experiencing in this present incarnation. You may be called to work with deities from pantheons with "closed" practices—rituals and rites that may require permission, initiation, or DNA ancestral connections. It is up to you to decide if you should partner with such energy. Above all, it must be done with respect.

The eight goddesses I talk about in this book come from pantheons across the world, so when we start to work with their energies, it's important to be aware of the issues around cultural appropriation.

Energy is energy; no individual can govern which energies speak to you. However, if you feel called to immerse yourself in a specific religion or practice after working with any of the goddesses in the book, I strongly recommend doing additional research and contacting culturally recognized organizations or practitioners of that pantheon. My advice as you navigate the journeys in this book is to lean into what feels right for you and honor the energies, and their cultures of origin, accordingly.

I've been lucky enough to form a personal connection with each goddess through divine synchronicity and soul connections, and you can, too! This book is just a starting point for getting to know the goddesses, so everyone will have different experiences of them depending on their own journey.

Additionally, you will see the word "goddess" throughout this book. However, be aware that many of these energies are not considered "goddesses" in their pantheon, or the word goddess or deity is not used as a cultural norm. The word goddess suits the purposes of this channeled text, but it is not the only word (or even the best word) to describe these energies.

Finally, all energies are unique in their own ways and you ought to pay close attention to your intuition and discernment when exploring them. If something causes you distress or makes you hesitate, don't give it access to your space. Remember, as a sacred being, you have ultimate control over this journey.

THE DIVINE ORDER OF THE DARK FEMININE GODDESS COLLECTIVE

The eight deities in this book are those who wished to speak directly to the divine feminine collective at this time. However, they are only a few energies in the Divine Order of the Dark Feminine Goddess Collective that are working now to liberate and restore balance to Divine Feminine consciousness incarnated at this time.

Other goddess energies that I have worked with as part of this collective include Isis, Mary Magdalene, Itzpapalotl, Astarte, Medusa, and Epona, among others. These energies are embodiments of different degrees of the fragmented parts of the original divine feminine blueprint, and their agreement is focused on aiding feminine-identifying people in activating, integrating, and accepting their suppressed feminine qualities.

Here is a brief overview of the goddesses and the dark feminine blueprint codes they will be activating in this journey:

- Kali is the Hindu goddess of death, time, and change. She steps forward to activate the codes for liberation.

- Sekhmet is the Egyptian goddess of war, vengeance, destruction, and healing. She steps forward to activate the codes for courage.

- Morrigan is the Celtic goddess of battle, death, destiny, and retribution. She steps forward to activate the codes for sovereignty.

- Hecate is the Greek goddess of the wilderness, crossroads, and magic. She steps forward to activate the codes for boundary setting.

- Inanna is the Sumerian goddess of sex, war, and justice. She steps forward to activate the codes for self-acceptance.

- Freya is the Norse goddess of sexuality, fertility, magic, and death. She steps forward to activate the codes for self-worth.

- Lilith is a goddess whose origins lie in Mesopotamian myths and Jewish folklore. She steps forward to activate the codes for autonomy.

- Tiamat is the primordial embodiment of water, chaos, and creation of all things. She steps forward to activate the codes of creation.

IN THE BEGINNING: THE FRAGMENTING OF THE DIVINE FEMININE

A Channeled Myth of Tiamat's Fall

In the realm where the stars twinkled in the dark expanse of the heavens, a silent storm brewed on the distant horizon. Far from calm, the world danced to the eternal rhythm of creation—a wheel of relentless power. Birth, death, and life anew. We, the observers, stood in awe as the Mother of All spun existence effortlessly from the void. The terror and beauty entwined in her transformative presence were awesome and terrifying. Brilliant spheres, ablaze with passion and ferocity, tore through galaxies, leaving trails of destruction in their wake. Matter bowed to their authority, and planets shattered into fragments. Such is the tale of Tiamat—the embodiment of feminine energy unleashed in a cataclysm of unimaginable force.

In the Beginning, Tiamat emerged anew from the cosmic waters, radiating with raw power and ancient wisdom. From another universal dimension, she was the primordial mother, the giver of life, and the embodiment of the creative forces that birthed the realm we find ourselves in today. Her essence, a symphony of contrasting qualities, blended fierce strength with nurturing tenderness, wildness with serenity, and boundless power with gentle grace.

While she was revered for many qualities, the power of creation she wielded was one that rarely went unnoticed. It both mesmerized and terrified those who beheld it. For what accompanies creation is not only birth but also change and death—a chaotic dance of particles colliding and transforming into cruel and loving forms, where rhyme and reason hold no dominion.

In the Beginning, there were those who, in their weak hearts, could not bear witness to the power the feminine possessed. The ease with which it transformed, untamed and unbounded, existing without dependence on external forces, struck fear into the very core of their being. They trembled at the unchecked power of the primordial mother.

Many seasons passed, as did many beginnings. From Tiamat's womb, she would create other lands and other beings, engaged in an endless cycle of birth, death, and rebirth—the ever-flowing wave of transformation. Until it came to pass that the one known now as Marduk, consumed by envy, rose above all others with the hunger and desire to declare himself ruler of all. With a solemn vow, he swore to dismantle the power of the divine feminine, perceiving Tiamat and all who carried the original blueprint of feminine energy as a threat to his dominion.

On the day they would meet, her new form of choice—a glorious dragon double the size of the moon—clouded the skies. Before all, Marduk declared his mission to tear Tiamat's power asunder. A deafening rumble shook the Earth, and dread cast its dark veil upon all realms. No force could hinder Marduk now, not even the gods themselves. With an air of entitlement, he lunged forward, mercilessly rending Tiamat's limbs one by one.

First, the heart of courage was torn asunder, leaving an abyss of sorrow and despair. The feminine could no longer stand tall, facing the unknown trials with unwavering conviction.

Next, Marduk turned his gaze upon Tiamat's limb of boundaries, severing it ruthlessly. Gone were the safeguards and demarcations that protected creation. The walls that defined what was acceptable and unacceptable crumbled to dust. Chaos seeped into every crevice, devouring the feminine spirit in its wake.

Autonomy, too, fell victim to Marduk's iron fist, shattering the notion of individual sovereignty. Each blow snuffed out the feminine's ability to traverse life independently, reducing her to a mere vessel for the dictates of society. The freedom to embrace one's true identity lay crippled and broken beneath the suffocating weight of conformity. Liberation, the sacred birthright to be authentically oneself, lay crushed beneath the yoke of obedience.

As Tiamat's lifeblood poured forth in a torrent of crimson, the cosmos became stained with her essence. Her being was desecrated and her wisdom drowned beneath a tidal wave of anguish. In his triumph, Marduk declared the firmament should be established, dividing the realms of upper and lower, light and dark, and with this, too, the powers of the divine feminine were split. In the wake of his domination and control, the sacred spirit of the feminine perished, its formidable force fragmented, and its original potency lost to oblivion.

Yet, with the turning of each season, Tiamat's enchanting melodies grew louder, transcending the winds, beckoning her daughters to rise. A grand quest for redemption echoed through the air, calling them to reclaim their suppressed power and restore all that was destroyed. Her emissaries emerged throughout the ages, each guiding initiates on a journey of enlightenment and integration so that the wholeness of the divine feminine energy may be restored.

This path is not for the faint of heart. Those who dare initiate into the original blueprint of divine femininity shall confront the demons that have haunted the feminine spirit for centuries. Amidst the chaos and disarray, glimmers of hope emerge. Acceptance, like a soothing balm, stirs within the depths of the collective feminine consciousness. Once buried beneath layers of self-doubt, self-value resurfaces, shattering the chains of self-sabotage. Sovereignty, the crown jewel of individuality, asserts itself as a resolute testament to the power of self-governance. Creation, the life force that surges through all beings, reclaims its rightful place in the hearts of the feminine, birthing infinite possibilities.

Tiamat's champions, those divine feminine energies who have been called "dark" or whose stories have been twisted to suit the narratives of the victors, step forward now as guides for all of you who wish to restore the wholeness of femininity to humanity and the Earth.

The divine feminine blueprint is not one of the fractured limbs and spilled blood but rather a symphony of harmonious contradictions. It is a kaleidoscope of strength and vulnerability, shadows and light, wildness and serenity—a breathtaking vision formed by the intertwining threads of intuition, compassion, strength, and sensuality.

So let us heed Tiamat's call and embark on this reclamation journey. In the depths of our beings, we shall find the courage to face the shadows, the wisdom to integrate all aspects of our soul, and the strength to restore the balance between chaos and order.

May the spirit of Tiamat guide us, her legacy a reminder of the enduring power of the divine feminine. As we reclaim our fragmented selves, we shall rise like phoenixes from the ashes, embodying the radiant light that flows through the cosmic veins. And in our awakening, we shall witness the renaissance of the divine feminine as it spreads its wings, restoring the world to its most authentic essence—a symphony of love, strength, and infinite possibility.

And so it is.

THE CODES OF
LIBERATION | KALI

In the Beginning

Liberation, the sacred birthright bestowed upon the divine feminine, lay crushed beneath the weighty yoke of obedience. Marduk, driven by envy and the desire for unchallenged supremacy, could not bear witness to the untamed flame that burned within Tiamat. In her freedom, she threatened the structured realms, where submission was heralded as virtue and conformity as law. Marduk cleaved through the limb of liberation in his ruthless pursuit of control, casting it aside like a discarded feather carried away by the winds of dominance. The flame, once burning bright, was smothered, its radiance dulled. And as the limb fell, the feminine spirit was left shackled, confined to the narrow corridors of obedience, where the winds of conformity extinguished the flame of individuality.

PROCLAIMING MY LIBERATION

I first stumbled into Kali when I began seeing the number 51. The number seemed to follow me everywhere in my visual field. License plates. Clocks. Temperature. Speedometer. It was 2016, and at this point in my life, the only thing I knew about repeating numbers was rooted loosely in the concepts of numerology and angel numbers. So I took a chance and looked up the meaning of 51 one day. The messages were interesting, at times extravagant. Things like "time to start living your purpose" and "step into your soul's mission" tended to be the themes, surrounded by other hopeful, yet vague, phrases like "positive change," "transformation," and "spiritual journey." And, while they all sounded good, they were super confusing.

I was in a mess of a marriage, physically separated, and considering divorce while working a high-travel job that kept me oscillating between extreme stress and pure bliss. Regret for marrying my husband, the constant triggers of unhealed childhood trauma from moving back in with my mother, and a feeling that I was on the wrong path had me feeling lost and confused, stuck in programs and pressures that kept me unable to make any sense of it all. It was clear that I had taken a wrong turn somewhere in my life, but it seemed impossible to figure out how to fix it due to life's expectations and demands.

Over four more years, 51 became more insistent, and so did the drastic failings of my life. I lost four jobs, four homes, a husband, and many friends in that short time. I found myself slipping deeper into despair and depression. I didn't necessarily want the things I'd lost, but I wasn't thrilled about living a life constantly flirting with homelessness and unable to provide for my young son. And this was when Kali first began to appear to me.

Like the 51s, her image just began to appear in random places. Suddenly, on social media I started to see posts about her. The name Kali would appear randomly in stores. Up until this point, I had never even heard of Kali. And now she was everywhere.

One day, clear as day, I heard so loudly in my head I couldn't ignore the voice, and I couldn't deny that Kali was trying to reach me, "I am you. You are me. It is time to let all of this go."

I would love to say that at that moment, I completely understood that all the continued losses in my life were for the greater good. But of course, it took me almost another year to realize that everything happening in my life was liberating me. To truly live my purpose and step into the life I had been trying to manifest for years, I would have to release all the things currently occupying my energy that weren't aligned with this highest version of self. My life was exploding, and Kali held my hand and guided me through the battle, helping me cull every shadow and unaligned aspect until all that remained was my pure soul essence.

Kali is the goddess of death, time, transformation, and rebirth. Walking with her, I have experienced countless deaths of different versions of myself. Whether we realize it or not, every person we encounter does not see the same version of us. As I began to heal my trauma and reclaim my rejected parts, I realized that the images people held of me weren't exactly who I knew myself to be or who I wanted to be. Fueled by the strength of Kali, I killed off those versions one by one, shedding the illusions of who I thought I needed to be to have the love and life I desired.

My journey to emotional liberation has been a long and winding road, full of ups, downs, curves, potholes, dead ends, and U-turns. On the way, I have learned many valuable lessons about self-care, self-love, and emotional resilience. I have learned to recognize when I need self-care and start with small steps toward healing.

I have also understood that emotional liberation is a process, not a destination, and that it is one I must continue to work on daily. I must practice compassion for myself and others, be mindful of my thoughts and feelings, and care for my physical and emotional needs. Sometimes, this means making a tough choice and letting go of people, places, and situations I genuinely love but which no longer align with my highest soul path.

Kali has also shown me how important it is to express myself authentically, ask for help when needed, and seek positive and supportive relationships. Ultimately, my journey has been one of healing, growth, and liberation. I am grateful for the lessons I have learned and the progress I have made, none of which would have been possible without freeing myself from the shackles of the belief that other people knew better than I did how I should live this incarnation.

KALI'S CALLING FOR YOUR LIBERATION

Kali Speaks:

"*O, my powerful sisters, I bring you these words of upliftment as you enter a new era of self-discovery and nurturance. Deep within you is unbound power, a source of majestic feminine energy ready to be set free. I am here to assist you in reclaiming this holy, untamed force, for it is through unfettering your doubts and restrictions that renewal shall emerge.*

"In your mortal existence, you fear the unknown, particularly the inevitability of death. And not just the death of your own human body. You fear the death of others' bodies, the end of relationships, and the changes of seasons and situations. You cling desperately to all that swirls around you, whether good for you or not, trembling at the thought of change. But let me remind you, death is not an end but a gateway to rebirth. Just as the life cycle demands the shedding of old, so must you release that which no longer serves your higher purpose. I am the herald of this death, the slayer of illusions and limitations.

"Within the sacred Hindu legends, you often hear of me as a fierce warrior in a relentless battle against demons. While it is true that these depictions honor my role as a skilled warrior, they capture only a fraction of the profound significance behind my divine purpose. Understand that my battles against demons extend far beyond any physical realm. They encompass the intricate landscape of consciousness, where the demons reside as manifestations of human frailties, limitations, and distorted perceptions.

"The demons haunt you relentlessly, their menacing presence weighing heavily upon your spirit. No matter where you turn, they seem to linger, ready to pounce on any hint of hope or courage in your soul. But these monsters have been sent as guardians of the truth—a truth that has been

locked away for eons, deemed too powerful to be revealed. This hidden knowledge holds within it the source of true liberation from the chains that bind and trap your spirit within cycles of dread and despair. Only by facing these demons head-on can the shackles of limitation be broken and your freedom be restored.

"For centuries, forces have sought to suppress women's power and potential. Ignorance has been used to perpetuate patriarchal systems that fear the unleashing of feminine strength. These forces keep women unaware of their boundless power by obscuring the understanding that demons are self-imposed limitations. By recognizing this truth, women can be liberated from societal constraints and empowered to rise above them.

"My soul roars with a burning passion for righteousness and freedom. I raise my weapon not to pursue conquest or domination but to liberate humanity from the shackles of oppression. Filled with righteous fury, I fight against these inner demons, crushing them beneath my feet as if they were nothing more than cattle. My strikes crackle with electrical energy and decimate anything in their way.

"These battles are far from mere entertainment; they define an eternal struggle to break free from the illusions that trap the human spirit, holding it back from true expression and enlightenment. Each defeat is an opportunity to awaken to the infinite power within your being, smashing through the barriers that contain and limit you.

"Yet even when I'm not actively engaged in battle, I am still present and compassionate. I, too, am a mother, and my love for my children of creation radiates throughout the universe, embracing every living thing regardless of gender, race, or creed. I offer this unconditional love, warmth, and solace to all seeking it.

"As you stand at the precipice of deciding to answer your soul's call, I offer my unconditional love and support in this journey of self-discovery and liberation. Enshrouded in these false narratives lies the key to unlocking the shackles that bind your soul and hinder your authentic purpose. I will help you recover the wisdom hidden within these tales, for they are not mere stories but potent catalysts for transformation. Let their divine light illuminate your path as you explore the depths of yourself. The ego's illusions have kept you from being who you indeed are, but it is time to break free. Let go of what no longer serves you and tune into activities that genuinely fulfill and inspire you. There is nothing to fear, no matter how dark it may be at times, as your inner strength rests there.

"Let the blaze of my energy consume the fabrications that have hampered your sight. Through this sacred transformation, you will ascend as a ray of brilliance, reclaiming your lost soul fragments, and radiating your distinct mission into existence. I am here to aid you in demolishing the falsehoods that restrain you. Acknowledge your spirit's deepest values and flourish into them with your life.

"The liberation you yearn for is not a far-fetched fantasy but a tangible truth within your grasp. Abandon all misgivings and cravings of your soul, and let us craft an anthem of liberty and ambition together. Unite in severing the false ego identities that impede your progress. Revere the potency of upheaval, decay, and the mighty river of time. Shatter the chains that bind you—the fear of failure, success, variation, and instability. Relinquish yourself to the mysteries with full force, as it is within this unexplored abyss where your soul's path awaits."

ORIGINAL BLUEPRINT
ACTIVATION JOURNEY 1:
KALI'S DIVINE CODES FOR AWAKENING
LIBERATION

In the luminous realm of transcendence, where the boundary between the physical and the metaphysical dissolves, I stand poised at the precipice of transformation. A hushed whisper carries on the breath of the heavenly winds, as if the universe itself acknowledges the weight of this decisive juncture. As I muster the courage to embrace my calling, a symphony of ethereal energies awakens, swirling and coalescing like vibrant ribbons of celestial fire within my body.

In the sanctuary of my soul, an incandescent radiance unfurls as green and gold rods of light descend from the heavens, cascading gracefully in a dance of divine intervention. Each luminous strand, imbued with otherworldly grace, weaves and twirls around me, intertwining in a sacred choreography of protection and guidance. Their vibrant hue, reminiscent of lush emerald meadows bathed in the first light of dawn, fills the air with a soothing, enchanting fragrance of possibility.

Within the embrace of these shimmering rays, a translucent cylinder materializes, encircling my being in a sanctuary of awe-inspiring brilliance. Its essence seems to pulsate with ancient wisdom, radiating an indescribable power that humbles and uplifts me. As I behold the intricate beauty of this radiant construct, my senses are captivated by the luminous carvings etched into its sides. They depict elegant symbols, enigmatic glyphs imbued with profound meaning, each stroke a testament to the cosmic tapestry that weaves together the fabric of existence.

I have entered the realm of sacred ritual.

In this blessed convergence of light and purpose, the wheel of my destiny spins, propelled by an overwhelming flood of energy that surges through my veins, awakening dormant potentials and igniting the flame of my most authentic self. It is a moment where the boundaries of time and space fade, and the infinite possibilities of the universe converge into a singular, transformative path. With each breath, I surrender to the pulsating currents, stepping into the energetic vortex of my highest potential, guided by the symphony of the heavens and the iridescent radiance of the green and gold rods of light encasing me.

The cosmic currents now aligned and the veil between worlds thinned, my senses are attuned to the subtle whispers in this noncorporeal realm. At this point of intense understanding, I am painfully aware of the sinister forces living inside of me, hidden away in the corners of my mind. They are the demons, the insidious guardians of my fears and doubts, who have languished in the shadows, scheming to obstruct my path to fulfillment.

Like tendrils of darkness, these energetic traps have ensnared me, entrapping my spirit with the remnants of old patterns and self-imposed limitations. But now, as I stand on the cliff of transformation, the time has come to confront them with unwavering resolve. In the presence of the goddess Kali, the destroyer of illusions and purveyor of change, I am ready to engage in the battle that will unravel the grip of these shadowy adversaries.

With every step I take toward the divine embrace of Kali, a determined fire burns within me, fueling my determination to transcend the chains of my past. I can already feel her electrifying energy coursing through the ether, her presence infusing the air with an intoxicating blend of ferocity and compassion. She beckons me to wield the sword of truth, summon the depths of my inner strength, and confront the demons that have masqueraded as my limitations.

In this container, time stands still. Shadows writhe and twist, their dark essence contorting in the face of the goddess's divine radiance. Here I embrace the holy warrior within, channeling the fierce grace of Kali herself. The battlefield is no longer an external realm but the terrain of my consciousness, where the clash between light and darkness wrestles, desperately seeking to restore balance to my unsteady soul.

In this present moment, I face the demons that have haunted my every step, their menacing visages distorted by the luminous aura of Kali's presence. Their grip weakens as I summon the depths of my authenticity and resolve, wielding the sword of self-discovery with unyielding conviction. Through the transcendent alchemy of this celestial confrontation, I step ever closer to liberation, embodying the spiritual warrior destined to transcend the confines of my limitations and emerge victorious on the path to self-realization.

I now invoke the sacred presence of Kali, feeling her discerning gaze illuminating me from deep within. With her divine wisdom as my guide, I take the first steps on a journey of profound revelation.

Like a veil has been lifted, the demons that once held sway over my spirit become starkly visible, their true nature unmasked before my awakened sight. I behold them with clarity, no longer fooled by their deceptive guises. These apparitions of fear and self-doubt, remnants of a bygone era, no longer wield their power over me. They are but illusory specters, whispering tales of restrictions that I now refuse to accept. The realization dawns upon me like the first rays of sunrise, igniting a fierce determination within. In the alchemical embrace of self-awareness, I dismantle their grip, one by one, reclaiming my power with every stride.

Kali Speaks:

"Listen, child of the universe, for I bestow upon you the gift of discernment. With my wisdom coursing through your very essence, you shall pierce the veils that cloud your sight. See, with eyes unveiled, the true nature of people, places, and situations surrounding you. Recognize them for what they are, and be no longer fooled by deceptive façades.

"Feel the tremors of fear and doubt that may still linger within, for they are remnants of a past that no longer serves your sacred purpose. But do not succumb to their grip. Bypass these emotions that seek to hinder your growth, for your power lies in transcending them.

"Take hold of the cosmic knife. Wield it with the strength that courses through your veins. With each incisive stroke, sever the chains that bind you, liberating yourself from their suffocating grasp. Feel the diminishing power of

these deceptive manifestations as they crumble before your awakened presence.

"From the ashes of their demise, rise and be reborn with unmatched resilience. You are no longer tethered. Walk with steadfast determination upon the sacred path that unfolds before you. In your every step, embody the strength that is your divine birthright.

"Trust in your discernment, for within you lies the power to dismantle illusions and forge your destiny. Embrace this truth and stride forth as the liberated soul you were meant to be."

Within the immeasurable expanse of Kali's ebony skin, my gaze descends into the depths of the unbounded void. There, I behold a profound enigma—the timeless space encompassing the essence of existence. Amid this deep connection, I catch a fleeting glimpse into the unfathomable vastness of time, space, consciousness, and creation. I recognize my infinite presence within its inky depths, just a tiny portion within the intricate cosmic design.

Yet this darkness is not a void of nothingness but a doorway to the boundless mysteries of existence. It beckons me to venture beyond the confines of my limited perception to embrace the awe-inspiring interconnectedness of all that is. It reminds me that I am but a humble participant in the celestial symphony, a speck in the vast sea of creation.

Kali extends her hand to my forehead, and her touch reverberates through me. With a single fingertip, she presses against my brow bone, unleashing an electrifying surge of energy. In an instant, the dormant energy center at my third eye bursts open, releasing a torrent of debris. The sheer force of this eruption leaves me breathless, my senses tingling with newfound awareness.

With profound skill and grace, Kali places her second hand on my heart while her remaining arms encircle me in a loving and protective embrace. It is a tender gesture, reminiscent of a mother's unwavering care yet infused with an otherworldly power that transcends human understanding. In this intimate connection, a sacred bond is forged between us.

Her divine presence enmeshes with me, and I am flooded with an influx of understanding. Through the portal of my wide-open third eye, the gateway to higher realms, waves of past wisdom cascade into me. Each fiber of my being absorbs this knowledge as if every cell were drenched in the elixir of enlightenment. The floodgates of perception swing open wide, granting me clarity, empathy, and an unyielding reservoir of patience.

Kali is now the conduit of transformative energy. Her cleansing waves surge through my energetic system, dislodging the attachments that have shackled me to a path not meant for my soul's journey. With each pulsation of her divine energy, I am liberated from the burdens that have hindered my progress, freeing me to embark upon the path that resonates with the very essence of my being. The radiant light of my inner truth now illuminates and guides me toward the horizons of my destiny.

I am now initiated with the codes of liberation, and I make my declaration of freedom to be heard in all places, spaces, and dimensions. I speak in the authentic voice of my infinite soul so that it is heard and recognized by all beings that would enter my energetic field.

I heal the wounds of the past and mend the hurts inflicted upon my soul, allowing the cracks within me to repair so that I may reconnect with my infinite source of light and become whole again. I quantumly weave a thread of golden ray energy so that this healing touches every physical incarnation that has carried the trauma wounds of oppression, suppression, and subjugation. The burdens my spirit has borne for too long begin dissipating, and I find solace in releasing and letting go.

Aligned with my Higher Self, I command the release of my ego's desires. I call upon the spirits of air to surge through me and assist in dissolving attachments one by one.

I release all excessive attachments to those aspects of the material world which have weighed down my spirit and have limited my Soul's freedom to explore new paths.

I release the bonds to toxic or stagnant relationships, which stunt my personal growth and prevent me from realizing my true potential.

I release ties to past events, grudges, and regrets that anchor me to immobility, preventing me from moving forward and embracing new opportunities.

I release my attachment to specific outcomes or expectations that restrict my acceptance of the natural flow of life and inhibit my ability to adapt and grow with the winds of change.

I release my dependence on that which is familiar, which keeps me from experiencing new horizons and personal expansion.

I release my self-limiting beliefs and negative self-perceptions, which weaken my confidence and block the pursuit of my goals and aspirations.

I release the need to seek validation outside of myself and the subservience to others' opinions, restricting me from expressing my true self and making choices aligned with my soul's desires.

I surrender ego's grip to inner wisdom. Clarity and purpose infuse my essence, birthing a reborn self. The old fades, replaced by newfound freedom coursing through my veins.

I direct the realm of the Akasha to release to my consciousness the wisdom of my previous lifetimes, as well as the collective dreams and hopes of humanity that I have shared before. This knowledge reminds me of my intrinsic connection to all beings and my responsibility to follow my soul's path, playing my part in this grand orchestra of existence.

I declare now that I am liberated from the cages that once held me captive. Doubts and insecurities dissipate like dust carried away by a gentle breeze. With each discarded layer, I step closer to my authentic self, to the embodiment of my passion and purpose.

I call to me the power of my I Am presence, which reverberates throughout time and space, to dissolve any beliefs, oaths, and contracts that bind me to stagnation and imprisonment.

I am free.

I am free.

I am free.

And so it is.

I now invite the presence of Kali to assist in clearing the energetic debris, purifying my light body so that I may emerge reborn, unshackled, and immersed in the radiant aura of limitless potential.

The tempestuous winds swirl around me, their force carrying the whispers of ancient wisdom and the divine guidance of goddess Kali. A flaming sword, ablaze with transformative power, is in her hand, ready to strike down the barriers that confine me. She raises her sword high, its radiant light cutting through the veils of illusion and doubt. With a resounding clap of thunder, she unleashes a torrent of blessings upon me, each drop a potent elixir of fearlessness and tenacity. I stand in awe as the rain of her grace showers upon me, drenching me in her divine essence.

Inhaling deeply, I draw in the essence of possibility, my breath intermingling with the winds of change. I am infused with the courage to embrace my true self, to confront the challenges that lie ahead with unwavering determination. The gusts of Kali's blessings propel me forward, empowering me to soar into the realms of self-realization.

As I stand amidst the storm, I know that I am blessed. I am chosen. I am ready to embark on this sacred journey fueled by the blessings of the goddess Kali. With her fiery sword as my guide, I fearlessly traverse the landscapes of my soul, awakening the dormant power within. The winds carry her whispers, the rains of her blessings, and the eternal flame of her love, propelling me toward my highest potential.

I radiate the confidence and clarity that Kali has awakened within me.

I am a force of transformation, a catalyst for change in my own life and the lives of others. I walk this path of passion and purpose, knowing the goddess guides and supports me.

In this initiation into Kali's divine codes of liberation, I embody her fierce grace and unyielding strength. I now close this sacred container with gratitude and reverence for the goddess and all the energies that have assisted me in this activation.

I am now a living testament to the power of liberation, blazing a trail of authenticity and empowerment.

And so it is.

THE CODES OF COURAGE | SEKHMET

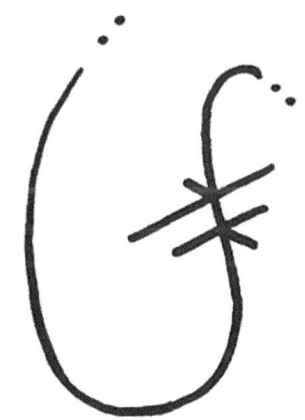

In the Beginning

Courage had been that resolute beacon that beckoned the feminine to confront her deepest vulnerabilities and forge ahead, undeterred by the storms that raged in her path. Envious and consumed by a desire for unchallenged dominance, Marduk could not bear to witness the unyielding strength within Tiamat's heart. The courage she possessed, untamed and unbound, posed a danger to the established order. In her audacity to confront the shadows and embrace the wild unknown, she was labeled as "dark," for courage held the power to dismantle the walls imprisoning the feminine spirit.

And so that pulsating heart of unyielding strength was mercilessly torn asunder, severing the threads of resilience holding together the divine feminine. In the wake of its dismemberment, an abyss of sorrow and despair unfurled like a yawning chasm, swallowing the essence of fortitude that once coursed through the veins of the feminine spirit. No longer could she stand firm, her resolve tested and tempered by the fires of adversity. The abyss of sorrow widened, swallowing the remnants of resilience and leaving a pervasive sense of helplessness behind.

FINDING MY COURAGE

I have spent a lifetime craving love and approval. At least, that's what it feels like. Growing up in an often chaotic environment filled with alcoholism and mental health issues, I quickly learned how to push my desires aside to make others happy. Navigating my family dynamics meant that I had to work hard not to cause any ripples in the pond, learning to be what everyone wanted me to be—a people pleaser. It became embedded in my psyche from childhood through adolescence and into adulthood; this deep-seated need to make everyone around me happy no matter the cost.

It took me a long time to understand that my people pleasing was the source of so much unhappiness and suffering. I tolerated toxic job environments, unhealthy relationships, and draining friendships—all to be perfect, seeking validation from those around me when I should have been looking within. However, as I put other people's needs ahead of mine, I felt increasingly drained and resentful. Though I was miserable, it took me far too long to finally realize that the people pleasing itself is what had kept me stuck.

The winged lion goddess Sekhmet began to invade my dreams as I ventured further into my spiritual exploration. Her dark complexion would glitter beneath the setting sun, her mighty roars shattering any semblance of hesitation that held me back from standing for my own truth. During this tumultuous period, I found myself wrapped up with a man to whom I was profoundly and inexplicably drawn—a stranger whose Tiktok videos and texts held me captive in an unfamiliar whirlwind of emotions and sensations. Whenever we communicated, I curled into a ball of fear and insecurity while striving to give off the right vibes to gain his attention and approval. Yet even as our connection grew stronger, so did my terror of being exposed as the not-so-amazing person I imagined myself to be.

I found myself caught between my desperate need to please him and the paralyzing fear of making a mistake. My stomach was constantly in knots, and my heart raced whenever we connected—both signs of the potent energy that pulsed between us. All the while, my childhood trauma lingered in the background, ready to swoop in and take over at any moment. My old people-pleasing behaviors crept up like a ghost from the not-so-distant past, refusing to let go until I could no longer ignore the way it was affecting me. I couldn't eat, sleep, or function. I couldn't manage to handle myself well; my neediness was choking me, and my emotions were all over the place. Everything felt overwhelming; our connection filled me with an intense euphoria I had never known while simultaneously sapping my energy, pushing me into an abyss of despair. No matter how hard I tried to fight it, my light seemed to be fading away.

One night, Sekhmet visited me in meditation, demanding I release the heavy emotions trapped in my heart. The goddess embodies courage and demands an unwavering commitment to spiritual growth. Working with her requires facing fears and doubts. True courage isn't the absence of fear but acting despite it. I realized that fear of rejection was damaging my potential and preventing me from living in alignment with my higher self. It was time to be courageous and communicate my needs honestly and authentically.

Sekhmet's wisdom, mixed with my own determination and willingness to take a risk, gave me the courage to face my deepest fears and admit to myself what I had been searching for all this time. Channeling my Higher Self, I composed a heartfelt letter that spilled out my innermost fears, wants, and needs from the thousands of lifetimes we'd shared together. As I wrote, tears streamed down my cheeks. Although I was anxious about how he would react, this wasn't just for him—it was an act of self-love and harnessing my inner power. After I hit send, there was a wave of fear as I waited for a reply. While I hoped and prayed my words would be well received (spoiler alert: they weren't!), I knew no matter what his response would be, I had already won the battle: this act of courage was solely for me.

One of the core places from which people pleasing comes is wounded and fragmented feminine energy—abandonment and rejection from people and situations in which you should have felt safe and seen. When you have activated your dark feminine energy and inhabit a space of unapologetic truth, you understand that you are worthy of love, care, and attention without having to change who you are or manipulate people into loving you. Restoring the original divine feminine blueprint codes of courage helps you in releasing the need to constantly monitor others or seek their approval. You have the inner fearlessness to show up everyday authentically as yourself.

The goddess Sekhmet gifted me with the codes of courage to speak my truth and free myself from silencing my voice out of fear of others' reactions. By embracing my authentic voice, I have experienced miraculous transformation in all aspects of my life. Although there may be times of fear and uncertainty, I know

I have the strength to stay true to my soul essence. It has been scary to walk the path alone, but knowing I can always choose soul alignment is a priceless feeling.

SEKHMET'S CALLING FOR COURAGE

Sekhmet Speaks:

"*Rise up and hear my voice! I am the one to whom the ancient Egyptians bestowed the title of goddess of courage and power. For too long you have been held captive by others' expectations of what your life should be and cowered beneath the weight of these demands. Now is the time for transformation. As your spiritual journey begins to awaken the dark feminine energy within you, I give my knowledge and guidance to help free you from such captivity.*

"*I have commanded the forces of destruction and war, yet I also bring solace and courage to those who invoke me. Picture me as a fierce lioness, adorned in vibrant hues of deepest red, bloodstained from past battles, yet walking forward boldly to fight in new ones. I am that part of you that nurtures those you love while simultaneously running fearlessly toward your own dreams and desires. Just as blood sustains the body, activating the bravery to speak and live your truth will nourish and invigorate your spirit.*

"*I remember a season in the last cycle when the Earth was in great turmoil, the sky dark and heavy with the weight of pestilence. The land was embroiled in war between factions all vying to control the fate of humanity. People had become lost and complacent, forgetting how to deal with the chaos both within their own minds and on the outside world. But then came the Ra Guardians, calling upon me to restore balance and harmony. I thundered across the land like an unstoppable force, breathing fear into the hearts of everyone I encountered. Everywhere I went, I was met with fear and trepidation. As word of my prowess spread, people's bravery increased along with their awareness and readiness. And amid the chaos, they found strength deep within themselves—like a river flowing through an endless desert.*

"Imagine, for a moment, this river flowing through the desert, the turbulent currents of life, where chaos and stagnation coexist. I approached it to quench my thirst, fueled by rage. As I lifted my hands to drink, the life-giving water transformed into blood, and my thirst for justice and retribution drove me to drink it. However, what appeared as blood was, in fact, an illusion—a concoction of beer dyed red. The beer symbolizes the intoxicating elixir of courage that gave those who drank it a newfound courage to confront their shadows and conquer whatever lay ahead.

"You might be tempted to doubt the significance of this tale to your mission of fearlessness. But never forget: true bravery is not only about achieving goals in the outside world but also having the audacity to battle your own internal struggles. Like I faced the repercussions of my

unstoppable might, so must you confront the results of your strength. It takes tremendous guts to take on the burden of accountability for the choices you have made, the aspirations you haven't achieved, and the alterations you need to execute.

"Hear my words, initiate, as they resonate from the depths of time and wisdom. The dark feminine invites courage to reveal itself, but this is not an invitation for the faint of heart. It is a summons to dive deep and uncover the strength within, unearth the bravery to confront the lurking shadows and fears of your innermost self, no matter how daunting. It takes a powerful mind and soul to heed this call.

"Know this, dear priestess: your journey of the shadow self is a crucible of transformation. Through courage, you shall emerge renewed, healed, and reborn. The willingness to confront the enigma of your existence unravels the threads of your evolution. Courageously embrace the unknown, for it is within those uncharted territories that your most profound truths lie. Confront the uncomfortable realities that reside within, and hold the darkness as an ally, for in its embrace lies the key to self-growth and empowerment.

"As you call upon me, you invoke the catalyst for your transformation. I stand beside you, igniting the flames of your courage. I am not just a source of strength and courage but a battle cry for justice and truth. Rise up, my vulnerable soul, and show courage by standing for what is right, even if the popular opinion is against you. Feel *the fire inside of you ignite, emboldening your conviction to speak up and be heard. Have faith in yourself that the sound of your voice will bring positive change to all.*

"Let go of centuries of shame and fear as you reclaim the dark feminine energy locked away deep within. Remember that courage is not a lack of fear but rather the strength to resist fear's power and move beyond it. Embrace your emotions, no matter how challenging they may be, for you must respect their majestic fury to forge courage from them.

"In the desert of your soul, let the sands of conditioning and self-doubt be swept away by the winds of transformation. Trust in your own power and intuition, for they are the compass that will guide you through the tumultuous terrain of self-discovery. Greet the unknown with open arms, for it is in times of most tremendous uncertainty that your strength is revealed. The boldness of your original divine nature empowers you to conquer any challenge that comes your way."

Original Blueprint Activation Journey 2: Sekhmet's Divine Codes for Inherent Courage

I step forward, crossing the ethereal threshold. The very fabric of reality shimmers and undulates before me. A subtle luminescence permeates the air, casting a gentle glow upon my surroundings. Blue and red orbs, radiant and celestial, descend from the heavens above, their hues intertwining in a mesmerizing dance. With each graceful motion, they spiral around me, drawing intricate patterns that echo the sacred geometry of the universe.

As they reach the zenith of their celestial choreography, a symphony of energy erupts into existence. The orbs burst forth in a cascade of light, manifesting as translucent domes of shimmering protection that encircle me. I am encompassed by their enchanting embrace, shielded from the trials that await on the path ahead.

A deep, rumbling voice like thunder echoes through my bones. I recognize the words as an archaic Sumerian incantation of protection. Its power seems to ignite a spark within me, and I can feel each syllable burn into my soul, like they are being carved from liquid fire.

As I recite the magical words, I feel a peace that surpasses all understanding. It's like a warm hug from an old friend. This tranquil feeling spreads through my body, starting from my heart and trickling down to my toes. It's as if I am becoming one with the earth itself. The more I chant, the more rooted I feel. Like a tree planted firmly in the soil, I am grounded yet serene.

I am now in sacred ceremony with the divine, outside of time and space constraints of any dimension or density. In this heavenly realm of divine connection, I stand with unyielding determination. Ready and resolute, I open myself to the challenges that await along my spiritual path, fortified by the celestial orbs, the ancient incantation, and the profound tranquility that permeates my essence.

Embracing uncertainty and discomfort, I embark on a sacred pilgrimage, aware that within the enigmatic folds of the unknown lies the fertile ground where my soul shall bloom and blossom.

I dare not shrink away from this path of fear, for it is only the raging winds that will harden me. I must face my doubts and shadows head-on, so that I may forge a new strength within. Though it seems as if these fears are here to weigh me down, they're actually torches calling me onward—they can transform pain into knowledge and wounds into something more meaningful. Thus, I stand tall amid the turbulent winds, embracing their alchemical power to push me toward change.

Like a phoenix rising from smoldering ashes, I transcend the limitations of my own trepidation. With every step, I am propelled forward, my spirit resonating with the timeless rhythm of the universe. Each encounter with fear becomes a sacred encounter, an invitation to peel back the layers of my being, exposing the vulnerable essence that lies beneath.

Come forth, Sekhmet! Your presence within me is a blaze of courage and strength that stokes the fire within my innermost being! My spirit is alight with your power, as I summon the fortitude to battle the forces of darkness in my soul. May your might carry me through this struggle, so that I may emerge victorious!

I stand at the brink of self-discovery, my armor shining brilliantly like a beacon of hope. I brace for the hidden secrets shrouded in fear and doubt that lurk within me, as I walk along the passageways of my inner world. I know that uncovering what lies beneath may be difficult to accept. Yet I remain steadfast and unafraid, for I am armed with courage, strength, and Sekhmet's divine protection. I am ready to face the veiled aspects of my being that have long held me captive.

Sekhmet Speaks:

"Courageous one! Let us immerse ourselves in the hallowed domains where bravery and empathy converge! Unleash the ferocity of your inner lioness and thunderously roar with the courage of a thousand suns. Awaken the flame that lies within you, entirely and without hesitation. It is this fervor that will empower you to embrace your true self unreservedly and create a life filled with authenticity, purpose, and sublime contentment. Believe in the fire hidden within, for this divine spark kindles your path to freedom.

"You must never cower from your power again as I, Sekhmet, summon you to ascend. Feel the vigor of your inner might surging through every sinew of your being! You possess the invincible spirit of the lioness that can overcome any obstacle. Every footstep moving forward shall be triumphant. Know that I am by your side, bestowing you the strength to confront your fears head-on and emerge victorious."

The blazing figure of Sekhmet reaches forth, her hand radiating a fiery red aura. She touches my etheric body, and I'm overwhelmed with a force that compresses at the base of my spine. I gasp in shock as I feel the tightness, all of the dysfunctional codes and convictions that have been my foundation crumbling under the unyielding power of this magnificent goddess. Her other palm wraps around mine, and she places a sharp, sun-shaped disk into it. Taking my hand in hers, she leads me through the labyrinths of my energetic system like an ocean tide, sweeping away any hidden memories and feelings that have hindered my courage to pursue what I want.

The ancient codes of courage awaken in me, radiating through all planes, universes, and densities. I arise as a warrior of the dark feminine, fearlessly claiming my power throughout these realms and across dimensions. My words are the proclamation of truth ringing out from all spiritual planes and cosmic vibrations.

I am now ready to willingly peel back the layers of conditioning and the discomfort head-on. Sekhmet's brave spirit guides me as I venture further into this inner maze. Her energy emboldens me to confront any darkness that appears and trust in my own strength to endure any storm.

Aligned with my Highest Self, I invoke the transformative power of the blue and violet rays of light, visualizing them penetrating and dissolving any energetic blocks within me. As I release and let go, I envision golden cords of light connecting me to divine energy, facilitating healing and restoration.

I command the release of the fears that have held me captive for far too long. I call upon the spirits of the Earth, my ancestors, and the souls of my lineage to assist me now in laying to rest the worries, anxieties, and distresses passed through the etheric cords from generation to generation. No longer will these vibrations keep our line in the bondage of self-doubt, yielding to the whims, conventions, and mandates of others, driven by the dread of assault, alienation, or retribution.

I release the fear of judgment and surrender it to the divine cosmic energy that flows through me. I bring in the white light of divine love and acceptance to dissolve any remnants of self-doubt and replace them with unwavering confidence.

I release the fear of rejection, allowing it to dissolve into the loving arms of the universe. I call upon my guardian angels and spirit guides to surround me with their comforting presence and uplift my spirit. With their support, I accept that isolation and rejection are nothing more than illusions created by a fearful mind.

I release the fear of criticism. I call forth the purple rays of transformation to transmute attachments, liberating me to embody my true essence. I honor my soul's path, allowing my true self to shine without worrying about what people might think.

I release the fear of punishment, surrendering it to the divine cosmic balance of justice and compassion. I surround myself with a shield of divine golden light that protects me from harm and negativity. Every step I take aligns with my soul's purpose, knowing that I am divinely supported and free from retribution.

In this moment of transformation, I invoke the strength of the Indigo Races, and summon the warrior within. I blaze into a pillar of light, unbowed by any force that seeks to subdue me. Now, I embark on this timeless ritual of empowerment!

I secure the gleaming helmet upon my head, feeling the weight of courage settle on my brow. It becomes a symbol of resilience, fortifying my thoughts and enveloping me in unparalleled strength. With each breath, I draw inspiration from the spirits of fire, ready to incinerate any challenge that lies ahead.

I adorn the breastplate, feeling its sturdy weight envelop my chest. With each clasp, I am encased in unyielding determination, a shield against doubt and fear. My spirit ignites, fearless and resolute, ready to conquer any battlefield of life.

I encase my hands in the protective gauntlets, their sturdy leather intertwining with my fingers. As I fasten them, a surge of empowerment courses through my veins, fortifying my grip on destiny's reins. For it takes immeasurable courage to seize the unknown, to face the challenges, and unravel the mysteries that lie ahead.

Securing the sturdy greaves upon my legs, I feel the grounding force of energetic roots anchoring me deep into the core of the Earth. I now draw in strength from the collective wisdom of ancestral warriors who have bravely walked before me, their valor and courage echoing through the ages.

With a firm grip, I seize the spear, a symbol of my assertive voice. Its shaft, firm and steady, reflects my determination to make my presence known. I raise it high, touching the spear's tip to my throat chakra. A surge of vibrant energy courses through me. A beautiful blue light radiates, enfolding me in its ethereal glow, while the cries of my soul's song reverberate in harmony. I am now infused with the power of self-expression, unafraid to voice my truth. The spear becomes an extension of my being, propelling me forward as a courageous champion of authenticity, emboldened to shape my reality through the power of my convictions.

I string the bow with purpose, ready to release arrows of self-advocacy into the world. As each arrow finds its mark, the world awakens to the power of my truth, igniting waves of change and inspiring others to embrace their voices.

Proudly I stand, armored and armed, a warrior of light, roaring with courage and blazing with sincerity, ready to conquer every challenge and fearlessly forge the path of my destiny. I am the unstoppable lioness, and my soul's roar echoes through the ages!

I feel the weight of my fears lifting, replaced by a newfound sense of bravery and empowerment. The old doubts that once held me captive have lost their grip, and the seeds of self-belief have been planted, ready to be cultivated with the caring hands of self-acceptance and self-love.

I am awakened to the understanding that true courage lies not in denying or suppressing these emotions but facing them with an open heart.

From the highest realms of my soul's dwelling, I summon the essence of courage in its purest vibrational form. As I receive and inscribe the ancient symbol of sacred geometry, cosmic energies intertwine, fortifying my auric field. With these symbols, I reaffirm the mystical bond between myself as an individual fragment of the all-encompassing source with all that is, validating my divine purpose as the architect of my safety and security.

Through the innate powers of creation, I manifest a sanctuary adorned with four planes of golden light interlaced with delicate astral threads pulsating with the life force of distant stars and cosmic energies. Within this ethereal cocoon of divine grace, I journey beyond the confines of the physical realm, harmonizing with the cosmic symphony that resonates throughout the universe. Nestled in the cradle of infinite safety, I am embraced by celestial currents of unconditional love and boundless protection, anchoring my soul in a refuge of serenity. Self-doubt crumbles across all incarnations of my existence as I embrace the fire within, shooting the newly activated DNA codes in energetic flashes like blazing comets streaking across the night sky.

In this revered connection with Sekhmet, I am initiated into her divine codes of courage, embodying her bold and fearless disposition. As I bask in the transformative energies, I honor and seal this sacred container with deep gratitude and reverence for the goddess, the ancestors, and all assisting forces that have guided me in this potent activation.

I stand now as proof of the transformative power of inner courage.

And so it is.

THE CODES OF
SOVEREIGNTY | MORRIGAN

In the Beginning

When the great limbs of liberation and courage were vanquished, an aching void threatened to consume Tiamat's independence. In the wake of their loss, she was cloaked in the heavy robes of meekness and submission. For Marduk knew that her sovereign power held within it a flame of defiance that would challenge his dominion. So with envy born of the need to control, he snuffed out her light, blinding the divine feminine from the truth about her force and trapping her in a predetermined fate. Tiamat could no longer define her own identity or chart her own destiny. Thus was the divine feminine robbed of her ability to exist freely in the universe.

RECLAIMING MY SOVEREIGNTY

For as long as I can remember, my life has been defined by one word: overachiever. I tirelessly pursued success, driven by an insatiable desire to win at the game of life. I knew the rules and expectations and meticulously crafted myself to fit the mold of what society deemed worthy. I possessed a unique talent, a gift of shape-shifting. I could become whoever you wanted me to be, concealing the truth beneath an illusion.

Life was a masquerade, and I had the masks to prove it. From a bubbly cheerleader to an "emo" outsider, then a wild party animal, I took on new personas to achieve approval and admiration. So I pursued degrees, scored top jobs, and even moved abroad. Yet all my reinventions could never honestly fill the void inside of me. I'd built cages of lies based on other people's expectations and judgments, and a societal narrative about success, desirability, and femininity. It was only when I finally pulled off the mask that I found true liberation.

Society has long dictated that femininity should be soft and malleable, a mere vessel to bend to its whims and fancies. The power of sovereignty, the ability to exist freely and define our lives without constraint from others, has been systematically demonized for centuries. Those who dared to embrace their desires and needs were often branded as unlovable, demanding, and undesirable.

And so, I tried my best to mold myself into the expectations of a "good girl" and a "good wife." Yet, despite my efforts, I always felt suffocated within this false prison, silently drowning in a sea of loneliness from disconnection from self and from others who never got to know the true me. I was lost, adrift in a sea of chronic unhappiness and depression. I wore a mask of perfection, concealing my struggles, for trauma from my childhood taught me that I better show the world that I have it all together and require nothing from anyone. However, beneath that façade, I longed for freedom. Freedom to live authentically, free from the chains of others' expectations. I yearned to define my happiness and break free from the commodified version of a fulfilled life.

One evening I was undergoing an intense experience with the spirit of mugwort. The room filled with the pungent aroma as I lay on the ground, tears streaming down my face while I grappled with a sense of all-consuming despair. My lips quivered in search of magical words; my voice begged for something, *anything,* to help me break free from this suffering of a life of suffocating obligations. In an instant, a powerful wind swept over me and illuminated the darkness. There stood before me the imposing figure of Morrigan, goddess of sovereignty.

She examined me intently with eyes the color of twilight, and her question pierced through my soul: "Are you ready to shift into a space where you are free to define your path to contentment?"

Exhausted and yearning for change, I summoned the strength to respond with a resolute, "Yes."

"So be it," she said, and was gone.

It would be nearly a year before I truly understood how Morrigan's energy was a driving force in restoring the sovereign power of my divine femininity. While the power of Kali was at work tearing down the structures that had kept me chained to my attachments, Morrigan guided me, peeling back the layers of illusion that had kept me imprisoned for so long. The path to sovereignty was not easy; it was marked by countless battles against the institutions and systems that thrive on conformity. But with each struggle, Morrigan stood as my ally, offering guidance and protection, fueling my battle cries.

Through the guidance of Morrigan, I have come to understand that true sovereignty lies in the ability to honor my own desires and aspirations rather than conform to external pressures. This journey has required me to dissolve layers of conditioning and question society's narratives imposed upon me.

When you are truly ready to fight for the freedom of your soul's expression, Morrigan comes to you, prepared to aid in your battle. Along the path, you will undoubtedly encounter resistance. The world around you will often fail to understand or appreciate the choices you will make on this journey. There have been moments on my soul integration path when I doubted myself when the whispers of societal judgment threatened to sway me from my chosen course. However, Morrigan's presence has been a constant reminder of my inner strength, urging me to stay true to myself and trust in my power. She will do the same for you.

Looking back on the many iterations of myself—the cheerleader, the sorority girl, the career-focused professional—I see them now as stepping stones, necessary detours that have led me to this moment of awakening. They were not lies but rather explorations of who I thought I needed to be to find freedom. Through shedding those identities, I have found the greatest love and acceptance within myself, and more importantly, the freedom to show up every day in this world as the person I choose to be.

MORRIGAN'S CALLING FOR
YOUR SOVEREIGNTY

Morrigan Speaks:

"Hail, Initiate!

"I come to you on the wings of ravens and crows as their dark plumage carries the whispered tales of liberation and untamed spirits. I am the Morrigan, the Warrior Queen, the goddess of destiny and transformation. Hear my call, for I am here to guide you on a path of rediscovering the hidden depths of your feminine essence, aflame with ancient power and primal wisdom so that you may break free of the patriarchal matrix and declare your soul's sovereignty.

"Amidst the inky blackness, where fear engulfs all who dare to tread, I am the undaunted, unrelenting champion of freedom and determination.

"Just as the moon gracefully transitions through its phases, I, too, effortlessly flow between various forms and manifestations to suit the needs of the task that lay ahead. My soul flows as it is called and, in this act, I express my divine right to explore the multifaceted nature of my being. This sacred right is not mine alone; it belongs to you, too. It is time to claim what is rightfully yours!

"My gift to you is assisting you in declaring your sovereignty, a mantle of strength and self-reliance. Just as I guided the people of Ireland through countless battles

to protect their lands and traditions, I am here to help you step bravely into the darkness. By reclaiming your divine right to express your soul freely and authentically, you assert your independence and take control of your destiny.

"Journey inward, and you shall find me there, a guide in the depths of your shadows. I offer my hand and the light of prophecy to illuminate your path. Let me help you shift into any timeline, drawing upon the abilities and gifts you need to break free from the chains that bind you in unproductive loops. I shall point you in the best direction, revealing the tools to aid you on your transformative journey.

"You are a mirror of the divine, reflecting the cosmos within your being. As you reclaim your sovereignty, you embrace your purpose in this grand universe. By living in your truth, you find absolute fulfillment and contentment. No longer will you be confined to living someone else's dream, following another's rules, or treading a path that does not align with your soul.

"It is time to awaken from the slumber that ensnares the collective consciousness. The crucial hour has come to declare your soul's independence, for this moment holds the utmost significance. Look around you and see the chains that bind society, keeping it mired in stagnation, illness, and complacency. The culture of your times has woven a web of illusion, perpetuating the belief that your purpose is merely to toil and produce, trapped in a monotonous existence bereft of freedom.

"*I call upon you to transcend this limited perception. Rise from the depths of this illusionary dream and reclaim your birthright—the right to live freely, authentically, and with unbridled passion. The world needs your awakened spirit, your fierce defiance against the status quo. A raging wildfire of ambition and determination burns within you—go forth and forge a destiny that belongs to only you! Reject complacency and declare freedom, the inheritance bestowed to all beings of this land!*

"*Activating your soul's independence inspires others, igniting the spark of awakening in their hearts. United, we will rouse the slumbering masses, stitching together a banner of total emancipation. Let us snap the bonds of homogeneity and fashion a reality where individuality flourishes, genuineness is revered, and the human soul soars skyward!*

"*I am ever near, no further than the beating of your own heart. I am the eternal fire that blazes within, the bringer of victory, and the warrior who refuses to yield to injustice. Know that I walk beside you through every hardship, for I am within you, always. All you must do is call out my name, and I shall be with you, lending you strength and guidance. But remember, it is you who must be my champion, for it is you who must face the battles that this life has placed before you.*

"*Now is the time to let your spirit soar, fierce and unyielding. Know that the darkness holds the seeds of transformation and rebirth. With me by your side, you shall emerge victorious, your soul shining brightly as a testament to your strength and authenticity.*

"In the realm of battle, in the dance of destiny, I await your call."

Lámh Dearg agus Croí Laochra

ORIGINAL BLUEPRINT
ACTIVATION JOURNEY 3:
MORRIGAN'S DIVINE CODES FOR
SOUL SOVEREIGNTY

I am infused with the resounding power that flows through the lineage of mothers, aunts, and grandmothers who fearlessly stood unyielding, their indomitable feminine might giving birth to entire worlds. The ancestral echoes of their strength reverberate within me, igniting a fire that burns with determination to reclaim the stolen freedom of our line.

The ceremonial container takes form around me, a vibrant fabric woven with threads of emerald ferns and spiraling vines, breathing life into the space. The pulsating energy of the stag, noble and wise, leads me through the veil of mist into a realm untouched by time's grasp. A silver moonstone, the ancient guardian of secrets, illuminates my path, casting its ethereal light. Within this enchanted sanctuary, I find solace and rebirth, shielded by the guardian oak, its mighty branches stretching toward the heavens. I surrender to the alchemical dance of the elements as whispers of wind carry my intentions, and the sacred waters cleanse and heal.

I inhale and exhale, my breath syncing to the universe's pulse as the energy of the elemental realm gently cradles my being. Each breath carries me deeper into the heart of the present moment, where time expands and contracts in perfect harmony.

The ancient rowan tree guides me as I stand in a state of alert tranquility. My senses are heightened, and I'm conscious of the energy and intention around me. The moss beneath my feet grounds me, settling my body with peacefulness. I inhale the smell of cloves, gaining insight and clarity.

I am now in communion with the divine. Within this harmonious sanctuary, I become a vessel of sacred alchemy, seamlessly blending the threads of intention, healing, and transformation. I am poised, embodying the grace and precision of a masterful artisan, ready to manifest profound shifts and weave new patterns of self-sovereignty.

I stand in awe, basking in the presence of the great Morrigan. Her power is like a falcon's wings, and her strength is like an unmovable mountain. I hear the echoes of warrior spirits, calling out to me from ages past. Their song of triumph brings fire to my soul, inviting me to look beyond illusion and reclaim my divine birthright. Like the crystals of old, her energetic field illuminates a path for me to exist—unapologetically and authentically—with the strength only found within my own soul.

Morrigan Speaks:

"Like a tempest, I now sweep away the false narratives and beliefs that have ensnared your being, clearing the path for the rebirth of your true essence. I grant you the valor to dismantle the walls constructed by others, freeing yourself from the confines of borrowed stories and perceptions.

"I offer you the nectar of mead and milk, and the sacred sustenances of red wine and meat. Embodying the pulsating life force coursing through your veins, they shall fortify your spirit as you confront the shadows within and nourish you, further igniting the flame of resilience within."

I take a sip of mead, awakening dormant strength. It grants me the audacity to face the battles that lay ahead. With each sip, the sweet and intoxicating liquid infuses my spirit with vitality, preparing my inner warriors to confront the spiritual adversaries who would keep me in bondage. It flows through my veins like liquid courage, igniting the flame of rebellion that flickers deep within my soul.

I take a sip of milk, finding the nourishment of the Great Mother herself, a pure and nurturing essence that cascades through my being, comforting and replenishing. It is the sustenance of tender care, the gentle caress of the divine feminine, as it soothes my wounds and calms my restless spirit. With its life-giving properties, the milk revitalizes my soul, restoring the delicate balance of harmony within. It reminds me that I am held and supported, allowing me to reclaim my sovereignty with tenderness and compassion.

I take a sip of red wine, sparking an invigoration of life force pulsating within my veins in this physical realm. The red wine becomes a catalyst, unleashing the vibrant hues of my divine soul blueprint, reintegrating my soul's fragments scattered throughout time and space.

I taste the red meat, and through its primal sustenance, I am immediately connected to the raw power of existence. This flesh is the lifeblood that runs through the veins of warriors, a source of strength and resilience. I am now anchored to the primal forces of creation and reminded of the instinctual nature within me.

My energy, emotions, and body are now strengthened! I am flooding myself with all that nourishes, catalyzing transformation, and celebrating the life-force that courses through me. As I consume these sacred items, I tap into my own power and open up to the guidance of my Higher Self on my journey to freedom and truth.

Morrigan stands before me, her presence resonating with the thunderous echoes of battle, her cloak billowing in the wind, reminiscent of raven and crow feathers intertwined. Between her and I, we are encased in a tornado of energy, the purest essence of the warrior, her eyes ablaze, reflecting back to me the fearlessness begging to rise within my own being.

Before me, she shifts into the crone of old, a visage weathered by time and wisdom. Wrinkles etch a map of countless ages upon her face, each line a testament to the trials and triumphs endured. Ravens and crows, her eternal companions, spiral and dance around her, their ebony feathers glistening in the sunlight. With each movement, they unveil more of one of her many forms. The old woman holds out the tiny stone, pulsating with the energy of the sacred Lia Fáil.

Morrigan Speaks:

"Look now at the palm of my hand. This stone of ancient power rests, emanating a resonance reverberating through your soul's depths. It symbolizes divine validation, a key

that unlocks the gateway to your soul's history and records. As you gaze upon it, feel the weight of its significance, for it holds the wisdom of generations past, waiting to be reclaimed by your eager heart.

"When this stone touches your skin, it awakens the ancient wisdom that lies slumbering within the recesses of your being. The floodgates of remembrance will swing open, illuminating the path that leads you back to the truth of who you are. With each contact, the stone whispers forgotten secrets, sparking a resurgence of divine power within your core.

"Embrace this sacred stone, for it is an emblem of your sovereign power. Allow it to guide you as you unravel the layers of conditioning. With its touch, you reclaim your soul's story, weaving a narrative that aligns with your most profound truth.

"Know that I stand beside you, ever-present as you navigate the battles of defining your existence. Receive this stone, recognize the wisdom it imparts, and reclaim your birthright of sovereignty and ancestral knowledge. We shall awaken the original codes within, setting your spirit ablaze with the flame of remembrance and empowerment."

As Morrigan places the stone in my open palm, I feel an electric surge course through my being. My fingers instinctively curl around its smooth surface, forging an immediate connection. A profound shift occurs, and my consciousness merges effortlessly with the multitudes of my soul's incarnations.

Like a tidal wave of energy, I am swept into the vast expanse of my soul's existence. Timelines unfold before me, unveiling the intricate web of paths I have traversed and purposes I have embraced since the dawn of my soul's individuation. It is a symphony of remembrance, each note resounding with the echoes of countless lifetimes. The weight of density dissolves, replaced by the weightlessness of pure awareness. I witness my consciousness in all its myriad forms, shimmering with divine light, untethered by the limitations of time and space.

Within this luminous state, the inactive spark within me is ignited, flickering to life with a brilliance beyond measure. Here, I recognize the truth of my being—a radiant, luminous being of infinite potential. The original blueprint of my soul, etched with sacred symbols and cosmic imprints, pulses within this spark, revealing the profound story of my existence. Thin, white fibers emanate from the core of this awakened spark, delicately interlacing through fragmented orbs of my soul essence. They weave together the wisdom of ages, a tale woven with intricate threads of love, loss, triumph, and transformation. Each thread of this complex network carries the data of my soul's journey, interconnecting fragments of experience and wisdom in a dance of perpetual expansion.

With the stone's touch, I am forever changed. The veils of forgetfulness are lifted, and I stand as a luminous being, empowered by the remembrance of my soul's journey. Guided by Morrigan's wisdom and grace, I embark on a new chapter, embodying the essence of my true self and awakening to the infinite possibilities that lie before me.

Morrigan Speaks:

"Hear my words and let them ignite a fierce inferno within you, consuming the shackles that have bound you for far too long!

"Feel the energy of Lia Fáil vibrating through your being. This stone affirms the rightful kings of Ireland, asserting their divine legitimacy to rule. Now, this stone is yours, a symbol of your sovereignty over your own life and your soul's destiny.

"Declare to yourself and to the universe that you are the true ruler of your existence. Embrace the blazing fires of transformation that surge within you, casting off the chains hindering your growth. Step boldly into the radiance of your soul self, for you are destined to shape the path of your own destiny.

"As the stone rests in your grasp, feel the ancient energy coursing through your veins, connecting you to the lineage of sovereign souls who have trodden this sacred path. With each heartbeat, affirm your divine right to claim your own story and honor the consecrated purpose that beats within you. You are the architect of your soul's destiny. It is time to build!"

My right hand lifts, and with the stone in front of me, I etch a single vertical line, with another in the middle, perpendicular to the first. The *beith* flashes in white-hot, golden energy that explodes into a ball of green, glittering threads that swell toward infinity. As infinite fractals, these green threads branch out like trees from their trunks. They extend as far as the eye can perceive, creating incomprehensible spirals, webs, and loops, carrying the weight of my words throughout existence.

I now swear my oath as the kings and queens of old have done. Let my declaration resound across the realms of both mortals and spirits, a profound testament before my revered ancestors and spirit guides. I proclaim my independence and activate the ancient codes of sovereignty that lie dormant within me. These timeless codes, etched in the sacred blueprint of the first-seeded angelic humans from the mystical era of Lemuria, now awaken within my very being. With these words, I pledge my oath!

Upon this Sacred Day, I swear to honor the energies of my lineage in bringing me forth. I am a unique being in this world, with an eternal right to freedom and self-expression. With each breath, I commit to dismantling the oppressive systems that bind me and the divine feminine. I take up arms against the force of evil as I call forth a new world where we are all honored and celebrated for our unique essences.

I resurrect my power.

I liberate my core essence.

I reclaim my inner throne.

Morrigan's soft fingers reach out to me and trace a *triskele* of glowing light upon my heart. My soul vibrates with the melodic frequencies of unconditional love and divine power that swirl around me like a cloak of stars, weaving together in harmony. And with each pulse, I'm filled with clarity, strength, and transcendence, until I'm enveloped in a brilliant auric field, emanating with ancient wisdom and healing energies. I feel the unification of my mind, body, and spirit melt into divine alignment. Like ravens and crows soaring through the vast expanse of the ethereal realm, Morrigan blesses me with her divinity, forging a sacred bond between us that inspires and emboldens me.

Reaffirming the sovereign brilliance of my soul, I now enact a sacred transformation, shifting shadows into radiant beams of light. I reclaim my divine right to embody the sacred feminine in all its dimensions, tapping into its profound reservoirs of strength, intuition, and healing. I cast aside the limiting tales that once sought to cage this force, understanding its intrinsic capability to usher in growth, rebirth, and unbridled freedom.

I reclaim my divine right to express myself freely and without apologies.

I reclaim my divine right to express myself freely and without apologies.

I reclaim my divine right to express myself freely and without apologies.

By the power of three, it is done.

As the sacred ceremony concludes, I stand in reverence, activated in the divine codes of sovereignty. Gratitude fills my heart for Morrigan's fierce guidance and the ancestral support that led me through this profound initiation. I embrace my path with deep appreciation and eternal purpose.

And so it is.

THE CODES OF BOUNDARY-SETTING | HECATE

In the Beginning

Boundaries were not merely threads embroidered upon the patchwork of existence but a sacred dance of self-preservation and empowerment. These ethereal walls shielded the inner sanctum, allowing Tiamat to courageously stand free, embrace her authenticity, and honor her sovereignty. But Marduk, in his attempt to become renowned as the most powerful god, feared the feminine claiming her sacred space, for within it lay the seeds of liberation, the audacity to reject societal norms, and the courage to defy oppressive structures, powers he had already removed from her essence.

And so Marduk severed the connection between the feminine and her boundaries. Tiamat's sacred landscape became a bleak canvas where the brushstrokes of external forces could paint their whims and demands. The once-defined contours of her existence blurred into a confused haze as her essence merged and diffused with the expectations of others. In this state of boundarylessness, the divine feminine lost sight of her own essence.

DECLARING MY BOUNDARIES

I grew up in a household where boundaries were a dirty word. From an early age, my sole purpose seemed to be catering to the whims of an emotionally immature mother who struggled to manage her own life, let alone mine. In this atmosphere of disregard, I internalized the message that my needs, wants, and limits were secondary to those of others. Before I could discover and define myself, I was inadvertently being erased, turned into a blank canvas on which others could paint their expectations.

This became my way of life—being everyone's anything girl. I was a doormat, ready to comply with any request, suppressing my discomfort and unhappiness. Did it matter how I felt? No. All that mattered was that others were content. I felt the incessant drive to try harder to need less, be less, want less—maybe then I'd have a chance at a happy ending.

The transition from home to the world felt like an escape. I found friends who seemed to understand me more than I could've hoped, but that didn't mean they had any intention of giving back the support I so freely gave. Despite knowing this, I stayed silent and allowed them to ransack my soul, fooled by the scraps of attention thrown my way.

Alone and in turmoil, I was forever lost without Hecate. I hadn't recognized her in the past, but now looking back, it was obvious she had been with me all along. Still, I remained stubbornly blind to her admonishments to change my life for the better. The painful exhaustion, inexplicable weight increase, battle with substance abuse, unhealthy relationships, and the false allies that surrounded me were all signs from her, urging me to protect my energy and choose myself. But rather than heed her warning that I must reevaluate my choices and take a new path, I chose to stay trapped in my darkness.

One day, something inside of me snapped after yet another argument with my then-husband. Fingers pointed at me like accusing knives, his words slicing through the air like flaming arrows. They struck deep into the wounds of childhood abandonment that still festered inside of me, sparking wildfires of fear and insecurity within. As I braced myself for another wave of painful gaslighting, I decided enough was enough.

Drawing on a wellspring of unbridled power and strength from a dark abyss within, I screamed, "Ya!" I'd finally recognized my own limit. A surge of power raced through my veins, a volcanic force that pushed me forward toward total freedom. With newfound determination and a divine breath from above, I stepped away from the house, never to look back.

Saying "no" became easier for me each time. I said no to people who wanted to leech my energy, no to masks I wore that hid the true me, and no to neglecting myself. Hecate stood with me at crossroads, guiding me and lighting the path toward being aligned with who I truly am. I discovered that boundaries didn't keep me from others, but instead guarded my energy and well-being. I realized that by setting them, I wasn't rejecting anyone; it was an act of self-love to prioritize and reclaim my power. With Hecate's help, I understood how to use boundaries to find balance in life.

I stood my ground against those who'd taken advantage of me, and those who previously enjoyed the spoils of my people-pleasing behavior weren't pleased. Hecate's voice was a soothing balm in my mind, coaxing me to reclaim my power and take agency of my own life. I dared to prioritize my well-being, set firm boundaries, and let go of energy-draining obligations with an empowering sense of conviction. I discovered forgotten passions that felt like home, and said yes to activities that made me truly come alive. Self-care became the cornerstone of my existence, and I said goodbye to harmful relationships without feeling any guilt or need for external validation. A newfound love and acceptance was channeled within.

Having faced my fears around the word "boundary," I have come to understand it as an affirmation of self-worth. I am empowered to make choices that are in alignment with my highest soul path. No longer do I feel obligated to sacrifice myself for others' gain. With Hecate at my side, I know that I can stand up for what is right for me.

Whenever you are ready to say "no" and release the illusions of self-sacrifice, she will hold up a light for your soul to see your gems that have been hidden in the darkness all along.

HECATE'S CALLING FOR BOUNDARY-SETTING

Hecate Speaks:

"Hearken to me, chosen one of the dark feminine. I call to you from beyond the veil and invite you to journey with me through your innermost being to reestablish your innate abilities as the priestess of your own spiritual temple. As serpents glide with purpose, keys unlock hidden treasures, and daggers slice through illusions, you must wield power

to assert your needs and safeguard your emotional, mental, and physical realms.

"In the untamed wilderness of existence, I offer you a guiding torch amid the enshrouding darkness. With its flickering flame, you shall navigate the treacherous crossroads of life, where a myriad of choices intertwines with converging destinies. Embrace this untamed terrain, for it is here that you shall unearth the understanding of your resilience and the unwavering strength within.

"Know this: healthy boundaries are not barriers that separate, but gateways that empower. They are the enchantments that preserve your inner equilibrium and foster harmonious relationships. Just as the hounds of the night dutifully guard their mistress, let your boundaries stand as flashing sentinels, warding off what is not aligned with your path and inviting in the energies that nourish your soul.

"Though I may be known to many as a mighty herald of interdimensional energies, this was not always the case. For I am the last of my kind—the Selunian—a race of starborn beings that once lived upon a version of your Earth's moon in its most ancient days. We were the protectors of cosmic pathways and could traverse realms beyond our own. But due to a fateful choice made by our collective, we began the extraordinary journey of ascension, culminating with the gathering of souls returning to Source. However, some chose to forgo ascension and embrace life again in otherworldly realms. After an age-long odyssey of my own, I eventually found myself in Tara, a parallel version of this Earth, where I experienced love like never before and decided it would be my eternal dwelling.

"It was here that I encountered other celestial beings, who had begun to be known as 'gods' by the local species of Tara. They were not from this world, and their unique powers were incomprehensible to human minds. At first impression, it felt like they came in peace to share their knowledge of energy and atomic structures, helping humans remember their lost wisdom and guiding mankind through its journey on the planet. For millennia, we all lived in harmony and symbiosis. I was mesmerized by this knowledge exchange, and I, too, began aiding tribes of humans in unfolding the mystery of the environment around them. However, as time passed, the truth behind these divine visitors became apparent.

"Beneath the veil of godly glamor, these other celestial beings harbored envy toward the depths of my abilities and the wisdom bestowed upon me by Seluna, as even though they had tried, they had been unable to establish their dominion on the moon. They wanted to use my strength and knowledge to serve their hidden agendas, yet I remained stalwart in my denial, refusing to let their nefarious intentions prevail. I made the difficult choice to stand alone as a shining beacon of resilience, an unrelenting symbol to others of what one can achieve if the inner conviction is strong enough. This is what personifies divine feminine energy—a symbol of resilience, determination, and unwavering dedication to protecting your values.

"*Drawing upon insights from the Selunian collective consciousness that still flowed through my essence, I fortified my spirit and honed my magical prowess. My heart burned with an unquenchable fire to safeguard the innocent and preserve the delicate balance of harmonic energy. I erected impenetrable boundaries that shielded the humans from the deceptive influences of the beings. I wove intricate spells that saturated the land with a protective aura, impervious to their cunning energies.*

"*In a great union, I embedded rubies infused with my own power into the sacral chakra centers of each human, activating their dormant faculties and amplifying their innate wisdom. These vibrant gems, pulsating with vitality, became energetic centers of discernment and intuition. As the crystals resonated within their beings, they acted as catalysts, awakening their senses to the subtle nuances of energy. The vibrations and cues that emanated when energies crossed their personal space became their compass, guiding them toward what uplifted their souls and alerting them to potential manipulation.*

"*In this bond between Selunian magic and human intuition, a harmonious dance emerged, where the humans became active participants in their own protection and growth. No longer mere pawns at the mercy of divine whims, they became sovereign beings, empowered to navigate the energetic realms with clarity and grace. When the souls of Tara were fragmented, the magic of the rubies followed them into your Earth, and the energy of these crystals still flows within your bloodline, an indelible* connection to the wisdom of the ancients. *Within your very being resides an internal compass, a sacred guidance system that illuminates the path when your boundaries have been trespassed. I offer you the key to unlock this dormant gift, to ignite your intuition and awaken your senses. Heed the signs and whispers emanating from your soul's depths, for they are the whispers of your Higher Self urging you to safeguard your sacred spaces.*

"Now is the hour to draw a clear line in the sand. Declare with conviction that you will not be pushed aside or disrespected. With every boundary you set, you show the universe that the unbridled feminine energy inside of you will not be denied. You are a goddess with divine knowledge and natural light—destined to receive all you desire. But never forget that you must listen to the guidance from within and consistently find the courage to act whenever someone, someplace, or something attempts to steer you away from your dreams.

"So, my dear initiate, stand tall as the guardian of your sacred boundaries. Trust in your instincts, honor your truth, and let the torch of your divine intuition illuminate your path as you navigate the crossroads of soul awakening."

Original Blueprint Activation Journey 4: Hecate's Divine Codes for Boundary Restoration

I stand at the crossroads, the threshold where the veil between worlds grows thin, and the whispers of unseen forces caress my soul. In this consecrated space, I will draw up the boundaries that safeguard the sanctity of my emotional, physical, and spiritual well-being. The air crackles with anticipation, carrying the echoes of countless voices who have trodden this path before me. With deft hands, I intertwine strands of vibrant energies and delicate threads of radiant light, fashioning a barrier that transcends the confines of this earthly plane. In this interwoven dance of colors and luminosity, I manifest a haven where my emotional, physical, and spiritual vitality is safeguarded.

I am now immersed in communion with the divine. The crossroads manifest as hallowed ground, acting as a grand altar upon which I place my offerings of honor and devotion to embodying my essential truth. Rooted in my inner power, I assume my stance as a radiant force amidst the whirlwind of energies enveloping me. At the same time, I anchor myself in the currents of protection and safety.

Moonlight bathes me in its gentle glow, casting an ethereal radiance upon my being, illuminating the secrets of the universe. Like a key that effortlessly unlocks the gates of destiny, I become the catalyst for the grand unveiling, turning the intricate gears of possibility as the doors to boundless potential swing wide open before me. Amidst this blessing of cosmic alignment, I seize my rightful authority to shape the holy outline of my life, directed by the mysterious power that radiates from the infinite darkness of the sacred feminine.

Restoring the Boundaries of the Maiden

Hecate, the ancient sorceress, emerges as a radiant maiden cloaked in shimmering moonbeams. Her flowing silver tresses cascade around her dazzling countenance, reflecting the soft glow of the celestial orbs above. Adorned in a gown woven from threads of twilight, she embodies an otherworldly allure that captivates the senses. Her eyes find mine, and like pools of starlit mystery, they sparkle with both ancient wisdom and youth's curiosity.

My inner young woman awakens from slumber in the presence of the goddess, emboldened by the vibrance she embodies. She raises a single hand to beckon me forward, inviting me to embark on an exhilarating odyssey through the labyrinth of time. As we begin this journey, an intoxicating blend of nerves and excitement fills the air.

I follow the moonlit footprints she leaves behind, and Hecate assumes the role of guide and mirror. The quiet confidence she exudes reignites my forgotten dreams and untamed desires, reminding me of the potential paths long abandoned. Her reflection echoes back to me the young girl inside of me, and I feel the rush of inspiration to reclaim my unyielding spirit, free from compromises.

We stand in a clearing in the wilderness, the brush encircling us, untamed, the light from a crescent moon shining above. In this space lies a calm lake, still as crystal glass. Hecate motions to me to look at the body of water. I peer into the darkness, and my heart swells as the reflection of my youth stares back at me, eyes brimming with hope and excitement.

Hecate Speaks:

"Oh, the naïve and idealistic spirit of youth! You can still feel that young presence within you, tangled in the threads of your parents' values. But do not despair; you may yet learn to embrace a vast world of exploration and self-discovery. Here, amidst bold, new paths, you will uncover your dreams, hopes, and deepest values ... just as you discover how to set healthy boundaries that honor them.

"The years of youth, when the world was so achingly bright, were marked by a grand unveiling of potential. However, if these moments weren't embraced with open hearts and wise boundaries, the shadows would hold you back from finding a genuine connection with yourself, others, and that divine spark of soul we all desperately seek.

"Together, let us rewrite this narrative. With youthful boldness, we shall create a new masterpiece with

wisdom and divine feminine power. Let us embark on a transformative quest where boundaries are cherished, connections are authentic, and our soul radiates like the brightest star in the night sky."

With a graceful flick of her hands, Hecate orchestrates a symphony of mudras, each movement a mesmerizing dance, weaving threads of moonlight into intricate energetic codes. The tendrils unfurl and gracefully seek out my waiting hands, their touch igniting a brilliant connection to the moon's enchanting magic. With the moon's power coursing through my veins, I stand poised to repair the breaches in my energetic boundaries that linger from my youth which have cast shadows on my ability to trust, nurture, and honor my being. Amplified by the essence of Hecate, my own healing power is now activated, and I can mend the fragments of the past and nurture the seeds of self-trust, self-care, and self-respect.

I locate within my energetic field imprints where the world's words and judgments took root. With a graceful gesture, my hand ascends, intertwining moonlit threads. Their agile, swaying forms slowly spin in unison, and the air around them seems to glow—first soft yellow, then a rich sapphire blue. This celestial blaze engulfs the dark gray attachment cords, each crackling and dissolving in a brilliant spectacle. In this sacred alchemy, I am freed from the weight of others' expectations.

I locate within my energetic field the spaces where remnants of vulnerability linger, echoes of moments when protection seemed elusive. With healing intention, I summon forth the radiant hues of healing green light and command a cascade of energy into each void. As the light permeates, it cleanses away remnants of insecurity and unsafety, replacing them with a profound sense of calm stability. Like sturdy roots anchoring a mighty tree, I embrace the deep strength and security that reside within me, knowing I am now the guardian of my being.

I locate the patterns woven within my energetic field, where patchwork disguises false connections. I now summon the full moon's power and shape it into a blade of blue light that shimmers in my hands. With steady strokes, I sever the fraying bonds of hastily forged relationships, releasing a shower of red dust. Every scrape stings like an open wound as I remember how seeking solace in others cannot heal childhood pain. Blue waters pour forth from the depths of my soul, cleansing and revitalizing me with divine serenity.

My hands rise, emulating the elaborate magic of Hecate in a hypnotic trance. As I move my fingers, the sacred symbols take form, shifting the fabric of reality. Into the Akashic realm, I trace my desires, and new threads of fate spin outwards. With each energetic gesture, the portals awaken to my will, reverberating across all of creation with a frequency attuned to me. Shimmering geometry and ancient glyphs appear in unison, healing my auric field while sending waves of transformation through space and time.

I ceremoniously declare the re-establishment of boundaries I neglected in my youth, this lifetime, and throughout all dimensions. In alignment with my Higher Self, I reclaim the power to identify what is beneficial for my being. I am no longer bound by the restricting forces of yesterday, but I firmly remain dedicated to nurturing the sacred space that is rightfully mine.

As the maiden, I embrace the boundless freedom to express my emotions authentically, unencumbered by the judgments or discomfort of others. No longer silenced by those who find pain in their own truth, my emotional truth is unleashed like a tidal wave, engulfing and transforming me forever.

As the maiden, I revel in the freedom to shape my own values and belief systems, unshackled by the expectations of family and the constraints of culture. Like a wildflower that blooms in defiance of predetermined paths, I embrace the untamed beauty of my journey, unburdened by the chains of obligation.

As the maiden, I bask in the glorious uninhibitedness to express my sexuality, untouched by judgment, devoid of labels, and free from the bonds of repercussions. Like a vibrant flame that flickers with unabashed radiance, I dance in the sacred realm of passion and desire, expressing the full spectrum of my sensuality.

As the maiden, I revel in the opportunity to chart my life path, guided solely by the whispers of my soul. I dare to venture into unexplored territories, following the compass of my innermost desires. I embrace the exhilarating truth that my journey is unique and sacred, and I cultivate the courage to honor my true essence and live a life that resonates with the deepest longings of my heart.

As the maiden, I define my identity as I see fit. I honor the truth of who I am, unabashedly weaving together the threads of my unique personality, features, qualities, and characteristics. I celebrate organic disposition and unlock the limitless power of individuality.

My intention is sealed under the radiant moon's light, imbued with lunar enchantment. With Luna as witness, my declarations manifest effortlessly, creating ripples of magic throughout the cosmos.

RESTORING THE BOUNDARIES OF THE MOTHER

Hecate's divine body seems to shimmer and swirl, her innocent beauty morphing into the powerful presence of divine motherhood. Her face is now etched with the ageless knowledge of the Creatrix and speaks of dreams made manifest. Her hair glistens like a starless night sky, cascading down in waves and creating an aura of serenity around her being. Clad in a flowing gown woven with threads of moonlight and adorned with symbols of fertility and abundance, Hecate exudes a timeless elegance.

The magical lake ripples, its surface mirroring the moon's gentle glow. I gaze again into the water, and my reflection transforms. The once uncertain, fragmented image of youth shifts, revealing a stable, capable, and balanced woman—the highest expression of my motherly and divine feminine self.

Hecate Speaks:

"The time of motherhood encompasses more than the physical act of bringing life into the world; it is about nurturing your dreams, passions, projects, and relationships. It is a time of deep connection, where your heart expands to hold the love and dreams of others while also embracing the expansion of your own self. Through motherhood, you become a vessel of creation, weaving together the threads

of your desires and the needs of those you hold dear. It is a dance of balance and nurturance, where your strength and tenderness intertwine to bring forth a harmonious life.

"As you create, remember that your own well-being must come first. You cannot keep giving of yourself if nothing is left. Let go of the fear of being selfish and permit yourself to nourish your inner fire. When you honor yourself, your flame will burn brightly and light up the world around you."

A brilliant ruby emerges in her hands, its multifaceted faces glistening with the perfect reflection of the moonlight. Carefully, she places it just below my navel—the energetic center where creativity, sensuality, and fertility flow—and I feel its fiery red aura blossom around me. The ancestral protection stone of my lineage is now activated, unleashing vibrant waves of passion, pleasure, and vitality that cascade through every cell of my being. A protective shield six inches beyond my boundaries wraps me in its warmth, enveloping me in a magnificent shield of fortified protection. As it pulses around me like the Great Mother's womb, I relax into a balm of self-care that revitalizes every cell of my being. This is a sanctuary for my true essence to flourish.

Ignited by the force of the Selunian protection crystal, I sever the bonds that have ensnared me within this self-imposed fortress of doubt and worry. I soar, untethered, toward the horizons that await me, guided by the wisdom and strength of the mothers who have walked this path before.

I release the energetic blocks and bonds that have constricted my spirit, born from the weight of overwhelm and the consequences of over-commitment. I shed the layers of obligation, reclaiming my time and energy. Empowered, I step into a realm of balance and self-honoring. No longer bound by the chains of excessive demands, I now prioritize my well-being and nurture my own sacred flame.

I release the energetic blocks and bonds caused by resentment from giving too much to the wrong people at the wrong times without reciprocity. As I drop the weight of unbalanced relationships, I reclaim my energy, restore healthy boundaries, and open the path for mutually nurturing connections.

I release the energetic blocks and bonds caused by the feelings of dismissal arising from ignoring my preferences and conforming to the preferences of others. I am suddenly filled with a powerful sense of certainty, knowing I can finally accept what I genuinely love and scorn what I loathe.

As I stand here in this sacred space, surrounded by the four elements and the divine source of life, my inner power begins to awaken. I can feel motherly strength radiating within me, spreading like a wave outwards. My hands move with grace and purpose, forming symbols of ancient magic, connecting me to the unseen realms. I am now able to open doors that were closed before, accessing timelines and pathways previously unknown. May this ritual bring forth new energy and deeper understanding.

In alignment with my Highest Self, I now restore the boundaries I have neglected in this life and all others where I have denied my divine right to advocate for my preferences, desires, and needs. I reclaim the power to honor and protect myself, cherishing the inherent worth of my voice and choices.

As the mother, I boldly assert ownership over my time, body, and energy. No longer will I surrender these precious resources to the demands and expectations of others. I recognize that by nurturing myself, I become a wellspring of love and strength for my loved ones. I utilize the power of saying "no" when necessary, as it paves the way for a life infused with purpose and joy.

As the mother, I am intimately acquainted with my limits and gracefully navigate within them. I set boundaries firmly yet lovingly, ensuring I preserve my physical, emotional, and mental well-being. In doing so, I create a harmonious and nurturing environment that allows both myself and my creations to thrive.

As the mother, I confidently express to others when they have trespassed a boundary I have set. My words convey a clear message that their actions or words have exceeded the limits I have established, ensuring that my boundaries are respected and honored.

As the mother, I recognize the importance of prioritizing my needs and well-being. By putting myself first, I can show up as the best version of myself for myself and those I care for. Self-care and self-nurturing are essential in maintaining a healthy balance and fulfilling my soul purpose with love and authenticity.

As the mother, I fiercely guard my way of life, shielding it from negativity and preventing others from encroaching upon the precious time I dedicate to nurturing myself and my loved ones. I create a sacred space where positivity and harmony flourish, allowing me to cultivate the life I envision. With love as my guiding force, I ensure that my path remains undisturbed and that my energy is devoted to what truly matters.

Bathed in the luminous glow of the moon's embrace, my intentions are sealed, infused with the enchantment of lunar energy. As Luna bears witness, my declarations effortlessly materialize, sending waves of mystical energy cascading through the vast expanse of the cosmos.

Restoring the Boundaries of the Crone

I gaze intently, and Hecate's transformation once again unfolds before me. Her radiant motherly appearance now assumes the form of the wise and ancient Crone. Lines of wisdom and experience are etched upon her face. A map of time, each crease tells a story, a testament to the trials and triumphs she has witnessed throughout the ages. Her eyes, deep and knowing, hold the secrets of the universe, reflecting the waning moon's serene glow.

The twilight sky deepens into an inky abyss, and a solemn hush blankets the land. The waning moon radiates with an ethereal luminescence, resembling the impermanence of life. Hecate as the Crone bestows her presence upon me. Her abundant wisdom and mysterious power rouse me to revere the passages of time, accept life's cycles, and find tranquility within the shadows.

Hecate Speaks:

"Transitions, deaths, new beginnings—these are the cycles of life, dear one. As the Crone, I embody the innate wisdom and strength that comes with age and experience. The storms we weather may leave their marks, but they also shape us into beings of resilience and power.

"Within the energy of the Crone lies the gift of visions, prophecy, and guidance. Just as the seed holds the potential of the entire plant within, so does the time of the Crone hold the culmination of all seasons and turns of the wheel. We carry the wisdom of lifetimes within our very essence.

"Embracing crone energy means embracing endings and accepting the inevitable. By accepting the concept of death, whether literal or metaphorical, we allow space for new beginnings to take root. It is not a surrender but a recognition that certain things must pass away for growth and transformation.

"Set your boundaries, dear one, and hold firm to them. Do not cling to that which does not honor your truth and desires. Allow the deaths and transitions to propel you forward, for within them lies the spark of rebirth.

"In the energy of the Crone, you are invited to acknowledge the fullness of your wisdom, to trust in your inner knowing, and to leap forward into the new chapters of your life with unapologetic feminine confidence. Surrender to the wisdom that comes with the passage of time, for in its grail lies the secret to your inner fortitude and perseverance."

She cradles a delicate vial containing a swirling elixir of deep purple hues in her hand. Singing softly, her melody and ancient words resonate through the air, coaxing the liquid to dance. With a gentle touch, she guides the vial to my lips, and I willingly drink.

Electric surges course through me, causing my body to tremble as the old ways of living die away. The parts of me that remained small, silenced my voice, and accepted anything less than the truth now transform into ribbons of light that swirl and dance like a million glittering stars. This sacred alchemy has unlocked my transformation. I am in perfect alignment with the Highest version of myself, radiating with vitality.

As the Crone, I honor the power of my boundaries, trusting the deep wisdom within me. I listen to the whispers of my intuition, knowing that it is a guiding force that leads me toward what serves my highest good and protects my sacred space.

As the Crone, I revere my personal wisdom. I trust in my own insights and understanding, recognizing that I am the authority of my life and making choices that align with my values and boundaries.

As the Crone, I gracefully accept endings that do not honor my boundaries, understanding that sometimes letting go is an act of self-preservation and growth. I welcome death to give birth to beginnings that align with my authentic self.

Enveloped by the radiant embrace of the moon's gentle light, my intentions are sealed. With Luna as my witness, my proclamations manifest effortlessly, unleashing currents of mystical energy that ripple across the boundless tapestry of the universe.

With this final declaration, my body turns to face the chosen path. The decision has been made and the die cast. No longer do I stand at the crossroads of uncertainty, for I comprehend that following the limits of my soul's truth shall forever guide me toward the rightful course.

The sacred ceremony concludes, and I am now activated in the divine codes of boundary declaration. Gratitude swells within my heart, an offering to Hecate for her guidance and the celestial energy of the moon that guided me through this profound initiation.

And so it is.

THE CODES OF
ACCEPTANCE | INANNA

In the Beginning

In his ambition to rule and enforce his power, Marduk refused to recognize the greatness of any creature as they truly were. His egoic force thrived on the desperate pleas of the masses, who cowered beneath his fierce anger. Tiamat's unrelenting self-love endangered Marduk's control of all creation. To maintain his authority, he needed to snuff out the flame of self-acceptance, which would leave Tiamat vulnerable to the opinions and judgments of others.

With a swift stroke, Marduk severed Tiamat's connection to the approval of self, slicing away the essence that allowed her to bask in the radiant glow of self-love. Like vultures circling above, the opinions and expectations of others swooped down upon her, tearing at the fabric of her self-worth. Without boundaries, she began to internalize the criticisms and doubts, allowing them to erode the foundation of her being. In the absence of self-acceptance, the divine feminine became a puppet, manipulated by the strings of external validation. Her authentic nature withered, transforming the divine feminine into a fragmented reflection, her inner light obscured by the shadows of shame and insecurity.

AFFIRMING MY ACCEPTANCE

For most of my life, I felt like I wore a costume daily. Despite the constant mask of composure, the reflection in the mirror showcased a woman suffocating under a mountain of expectations—both self-imposed and external. It's as if, from birth, I was coded with the belief that my very existence was an inconvenience. Existential shame was all I knew, and it was a full-time job to avoid experiencing the pain of feeling like I didn't deserve to have a space on this planet.

I grew up around caregivers who, despite their best intentions, gave me a skewed perspective of my worth. I knew my duty was to maintain a perfect image to survive in my environment. Any criticism or reprimand felt like a personal attack instead of a lesson to be learned. It became clear that no matter what I did, an underlying fear would always be lingering in my heart—the fear of being an unlovable mess.

Around the time I began my initiation into the High Priestess path, my son's autism diagnosis and unexpected divorce were hard blows that kept reverberating throughout my life, making it hard to maintain relationships with people who constantly judged me for my choices. No matter how much I tried to put on a brave face and make excuses for myself and the things I perceived that I had lost, the weight of the façade became too heavy to bear.

Of course, sometimes I seemed to transcend this fear and speak my truth from my soul, consequences be damned. In these moments, waves of molten energy would flood through me as if I were tapping into a golden solar reservoir. But they would fade as quickly as they came. I continued to find myself overwhelmed by feelings of inadequacy and loneliness everywhere I turned, wanting nothing more than a moment to feel genuinely accepted.

One night, as I absentmindedly scrolled through TikTok, my mind churned in its usual cycle of turbulent thoughts bouncing between self-loathing and self-improvement. A comment about the Sumerians on one of my light language videos caught my eye, making me pause to read further. Curiosity piqued, I felt pulled to explore myths of this lost civilization. Specifically, Inanna's descent into the Underworld. As I read, the same waves of warm energy flooded through me, just as they had other times when I had been in alignment with voicing my truth.

I could feel the searing pain of my own struggles tangled in my chest as I related to Inanna's battle to find peace within herself through periods of loss, judgment, and self-reflection. Here she was, a powerful goddess draped with gold and jewels, a skilled warrior adored by thousands, yet she yearned for something more. The longing to be accepted by the other gods landed her in the Underworld, deceived and stripped of her comforts by those she called family, alone and abandoned, while those who claimed they loved her—even her father and husband—left her dead in the world of shadows. In her darkest moment, Inanna had to face the truth: the only will that mattered was her own. Once she accepted the fullness of her power, blemishes and all, she was able to separate the false lights of people who would never view her as the divine feminine goddess she truly was from those true soul connections who only wanted to help her thrive.

As I sat there, the realization hit me like an unexpected gust of wind. I no longer needed to creep in the shadows, hiding who I was or what I had been through out of fear of what others thought of me. My imperfections were not a source of shame but strengths that added depth and nuance to my identity. Life would bring challenges, but I could meet them with newfound power rooted in accepting them and myself for what we were. The lighthouse within me was lit, guiding me toward new horizons.

First, I shed the trappings of education and external validation that I had used to buffer against the rejection of my feelings and emotions. No diploma or approval from anyone else mattered compared to my power to define who I was and what I knew to be true. I realized that only I held the authority to be who I wanted to be and to define my reality.

Next, I released the overpowering grip of societal standards as the judgment of my beauty that I had used as the benchmark of worthiness. I relished the liberating truth that they were never designed for me. Instead of succumbing to those expectations, I welcomed and celebrated the uneven curves of my body, shaped by time and motherhood. My dark brown skin glowed with joy and became a symbol of power and resilience, rejecting all restricted definitions of beauty imposed on women.

But above all, I deconstructed the concept of femininity that I believed I needed to embody to be safe and loved in the world. I unearthed the depths of my dark feminine energy, unlocking a kaleidoscope of strength and courage. Like Inanna standing before the Annuna without her garments, I shrugged off society's shackles and bravely faced any judgment as the most genuine version of myself. My femininity no longer demanded softness and conformity; it resonated with sharpness, confidence, and charisma. It was messy, impulsive, and unapologetically opinionated. No longer shying away from my flaws, I wore them proudly and gloried in the freedom of being wholly me. I stood in the full bloom of authenticity.

Inanna's journey was not without peril; she faced difficult obstacles as she traversed through the Underworld, ultimately losing possessions and identity as she descended. My journey toward acceptance has been no different. The crusade to accept who I was at my soul's core repeatedly reminded me that I had no clue who I was. Ultimately, Inanna emerged from the Underworld more powerful than ever before, having gained a greater sense of self-knowledge and acceptance along her journey. And this is what she did for me, continuously pushing me forward to remove the layers of veneer that I had used to gloss over my true self.

I am still learning to embrace my own struggles with acceptance. Luckily, Inanna is ever-present, reminding me that these tests will become my most profound teachers if I confront obstacles head-on. She is an icon of strength and poise for all women facing societal pressures or the challenge of changing definitions of beauty and success. We can discover true greatness within ourselves by accepting our unique journeys completely.

Inanna Calling for Your Acceptance

Inanna Speaks:

"Many attempts to explain me have been made, but they all fail. My influence is too complex for any one narrative or mortal mind to contain it. Even the gods are taken aback by my vigor. In all their omnipotence, they cannot

control me. Human minds cannot fully comprehend my existence; I defy comprehension and confinement, stretching for eternity.

"I was the child of two worlds. Though a stranger to the soil, I claimed it as my home, as my family had done for eons before me. In this incarnation, my people were from Nibiru, a distant realm outside of this universe's golden solar bracket. Many cycles ago, our family decided to settle in this realm on a quest to save our home. Yet, after three generations of settlements on Ki, there was still an invisible line dividing those of us who hailed from heaven and the humans. We felt obligated to represent ourselves as gods and uphold our superiority with every interaction, the mission from high we were sworn to fulfill. The energy of the two intermingling cultures always surrounded me, forcing me to choose which legacy I wanted to follow.

"Growing up, I felt like a caged bird among the Annunaki females who wished to suppress my spirit and hitch it to their supposed rules of status, order, lineage, and propriety. But when I would venture down to the land below where the humans were, I felt liberated with every breath taken. The Abzu was alive with vibrant people who had taught me that love was not bound by societal borders but could encompass us all in its warmth. Every night these irrepressible souls filled the air with their laughter, music, and at times, even their tears as they held each other close. Knowing they were free spirits set ablaze made me ready to rebel against any rule that sought to confine me.

"My grandfather had made it his life's work to harness the power of humanity, but no matter how hard he tried, their spirit could never be extinguished. Even in the face of subjugation, they still held onto their hope. The resiliency of mankind proved so great that it could never be contained, despite my grandfather's best efforts to manipulate and exploit them. I deeply admired their resolve and spirit.

"Within them, I recognized the very essence that burned within me—the yearning for freedom, the desire to live by my own rules and creeds rather than bowing to the expectations and impositions of those who viewed us as mere pawns in a game of control and domination.

"I adopted their ways as I spent more time among humans in the Abzu. I strode through heaven without veils, unashamed of my form. I spoke boldly about conditions in the different Regions, using my voice as a horn against injustice. Attempts to silence or admonish me were met with laughter, for I knew that I, too, was a divinely crafted spark of the feminine, created in perfection just as I was. I did not need to heed the dictates and decrees that sought to define and confine me.

"My choices may have been unwise, but they were my own. Regret has been an unwelcome friend of mine, yet even through the most challenging moments, I never forgot that I was the only one responsible for my decisions. No matter what those around me think or say, I take ownership of the consequences of my actions, however severe they may be. Never once have I claimed innocence when I was wrong;

I saw every negative cause and effect as an opportunity to grow. While those closest to me have chosen to cast their judgment and spite at me out of self-serving interests, I decided to accept my nature without excuse or apology, loving my flaws and faults just as fiercely as they are condemned. Instead of allowing fate to take its course, I have taken charge of my life choices and held sway over my destiny.

"People often tell the tale of when I descended to the Lower Worlds to visit my sister, Ereshkigal. I wanted nothing more than to mend our discontent and aid her through her grief for her lost husband. Nevertheless, I faced unjust criticism and prejudice at every step of my journey. The underworld sentinels commanded that all symbols of power and authority be relinquished before they granted me access, stripping me of any signs of wealth or nobility. Jewelry, crowns, clothes—even the sacred MEs—were taken away from me in this quest. Despite all these setbacks, not even their scorn could hold me back; I still possessed an undeniable strength within myself.

"Even as the Annuna tried to break and humiliate me, I refused to be moved. Naked before those who would judge me, I never once bowed my head in shame or regret. I stripped away all the façades, masks, and personas I had used to define myself. In the Lower World, I stared down danger and despair and emerged victorious—a feat few could claim. Now it is my turn to guide you through your journey of self-acceptance, where you will find a strength that far surpasses any external validation. It lies beneath

the surface, beyond the clutches of judgment and fear. In self-acceptance lives a source of courage that stems from the divine knowledge that you remain worthy and whole even in the darkness of your soul. And as you embrace your inner power, nothing can hold you back.

"I stand before you now, my sisters, to remind you that becoming comfortable in your skin is a bold act of rebellion. It is your birthright to love yourself and strive for acceptance without apology. The people around you may try to fashion themselves as gods. They may try to convince you that you are inferior. But remember: we are all expressions of the same Source Creator. We are part of one, unified by our common spiritual essence. This realization helps us resist the urge to compete with each other and instead accept one another with open hearts and minds.

"Oh, dearest initiate! Shed the doubt that holds you back like a worn-out garment. Be brave enough to stand in your truth, knowing that all missteps and imperfections make you the unique human expression of your soul. Own your quirks, scars, and beauty. Let your true self shine through every part of you. Then, own your capabilities, rise to your true potential, and express yourself with unadulterated confidence!

"Above all else, remember that self-acceptance is a journey of perseverance and relentless love. With courage and compassion, you will discover your true power by listening to the wisdom of your intuition. Though the path ahead may be twisted and marked with fear, never forget that

I am standing beside you—a source of strength and encouragement as you navigate this terrain of self-love and appreciation.

"May your path be illuminated by the Morning and Evening star's light so that you may soon dance freely and fiercely upon the reverent canvas of life."

ORIGINAL BLUEPRINT
ACTIVATION JOURNEY 5:
INANNA'S DIVINE CODES FOR RADICAL
SELF-ACCEPTANCE

I stand at the gates to my personal underworld, a realm cloaked in shadows where the essence of fate and judgment fills the thick air. As I approach, a chill envelopes me, prickling my skin like ethereal fingertips. The atmosphere is heavy with anticipation, carrying an otherworldly scent that mingles hints of ancient parchment and smoldering incense, creating an intoxicating aroma that wafts through the corridors of destiny.

For too long I've forgotten heaven, neglecting the divine harmony it offers to my soul and the serenity found in accepting my personal truths.

For too long I've clung to Earth, desperately entwined in the illusory grasp of worldly pursuits, caught in an endless cycle of pursuing false idols, hoping they would grant me a sense of groundedness, stability, and self-worth.

In this moment, I descend into the depths of the underworld, fearlessly confronting my inner demons and shadows. With open arms, I embrace judgment, taking ownership of my choices, ready for rebirth into my feminine essence, unburdened by shame.

I open myself to divine presence and feel a gentle breeze caress my skin, bringing with it the fragrant aroma of vanilla, amber, and rose, a sign that the goddess Inanna has arrived. Though I cannot see her form, a beautiful melody carries through this sacred space, stirring my soul and beckoning me onward. In this moment, time stands still as boundaries between us dissolve and I become both myself and her—inseparable, whole.

I am me, yet I am she, and we are one.

Through this divine communion, I enter the sacred enclave of ceremony, enveloped by the protective embrace of the goddess. I exist as an individual, yet indistinguishable from her essence—we are united as a singular embodiment of divine power and grace. The melding of our energies nurtures and shields me, forever entwined in glorious harmony.

I am me, yet I am she, and we are one.

In the abyss of the pitch-black night, a small orb emerges, drawing my attention. Ninsi'anna, Venus herself, my guardian angel of light, stands alone in the heavens. In the abyss of the pitch-black night, a small orb emerges, drawing my attention. The light she unleashes illuminates all around, painting the world in exquisite rays of shimmering hues. I am awed by her glorious radiance and give thanks for the wondrous magic she has bestowed.

The rays narrow into a circular mirror, and I behold my form, draped in the regalia of the Sumerians of the Olden Times. Adorning my head is a golden crown, its majestic curves and shimmering embellishments projecting strength, restraint, and the weight of responsibility. The touch of its smooth metal against my brow reminds me of the noble authority it bestows.

Gracing my throat is a lapis lazuli necklace, its vibrant blue hues captivating the eye. Each intricately crafted bead, glistening like fragments of the sky, communicates my elevated status with silent eloquence. As I run my fingers along its cool surface, I am reminded of the prestige and esteem it carries. Three delicate gold bracelets give a soft jingle with the movement of my arm, their sound the only audible note in the sea of silence.

A flowing gown drapes upon my figure, its fabric testament to the desirable, gentle, feminine allure. It glides over my skin in delicate caresses, the embodiment of grace and elegance.

Strewn across my shoulders and chest, velvety robes envelop me. Their deep, velveteen folds exude a sense of modesty and purity, their weight a constant reminder of the reverence that befits my presence.

Adorning my left hand, a golden ring of exquisite craftsmanship glimmers and sparkles, reflecting the light with its enchanting radiance. Its delicate engravings tell a story of beauty and significance, displayed for all to see.

In my right hand, I tightly grip a staff bejeweled with lapis lazuli, its vivid blue hues resonating with an otherworldly energy. This staff, like a trusted companion, supports me and keeps me in line. Etched upon the weathered surface of the staff, intricate markings of measurement create a mesmerizing tapestry, each line and symbol holding the weight of history. They speak of journeys taken, boundaries crossed, and lessons learned. As I run my fingers over these sacred carvings, a sense of reverence washes over me, grounding me in purpose and reminding me of the eternal flow of time.

From the depths of shadows I've tried to deny, I call forth a circle of seven gates that unfold in a circle around me. Standing in their midst, I feel the energies emanating from them like unseen hands weaving webs of illusion and trickery from malevolent paths that attempt to lead me astray.

Though apprehension lurks within me, courage imbues my spirit and guides me forward. My life's journey is no longer something to fear, but an opportunity for inner transformation and self-acceptance. I offer up this prayer to Inanna—the goddess of power within me—beckoning her blessing as I traverse the mysterious realms of my soul's underworld.

As I walk toward the first gate, the wrought iron doors seem to tower over me menacingly, as if they are about to spring to life and snatch away whatever I offer. After removing the crown from my head, I place it gently at its base, leaving behind the restraints of imposed responsibilities before I proceed to its partner. At the second gate, I remove my lapis-lazuli necklace and drop it delicately at the threshold, silently kissing away the illusion of peace status seemed to bring.

Without hesitation, I move swiftly on to the third and fourth gates, adding my ring and bracelets, releasing the use of the beauty of my physical form to seek acceptance from others. Dread fills me as I move to the fifth gate. I bow before it, leaving my staff at its ground, daring to walk forward without looking to the clear lines set up by societal expectations to guide me. I undo the clasp of my robe, letting it slide off me gracefully at the sixth gate, before moving to the seventh gate and removing my gown. Gone now are the pretenses and narrow definitions of femininity marked by false modesty. One by one the layers have been discarded and there is nothing left but me standing naked like Inanna herself, ready for whatever awaits behind those doors.

Allowing the full power of Inanna to course through my body, I speak:

I make my declaration to all in this underworld. To spirits of entities that would keep me trapped here with them and to the ancestors who rage with jealousy and contempt for missions they were not able to complete. Hear my words and let this decree break these cords and contracts!

I release the tightly clenched grip of control, dissolving the illusion that binds me. Embracing the vast unknown, I trust in the divine plan of life's unfolding, guided by the whispers of my Highest Self. No longer confined by the rigid walls of conformity, I break free from the templates of social conditioning. The misaligned beliefs of family and culture lose their grip on my spirit as I reclaim my sovereignty. The dictations of how my life should be fade into insignificance, their influence dissolved by the winds of liberation.

Without control, I love and accept myself.

I release the chain that constricts my voice, liberating the power to express my truth. No longer shall I mask profound emotions with superficial adornments that diminish their significance. I embrace authenticity, wielding words that flow forth with fairness and honesty, releasing the unfiltered truth of my soul into the world.

Without fictions, I love and accept myself.

I release the heavy weight of needing to show that I am valuable through material possessions. I spread my wings of authenticity and find freedom from these temporary items. No longer will I feel like I have to buy things to be seen as worthy. Instead, I start exploring myself and realize that the worth I own is within me, not in what I own. With grace and humility, I show who I truly am and trust that my personality and spirit will lead me forward.

Without emblems, I love and accept myself.

I release the need to compare myself to others, relinquishing the chains that bind my spirit. No longer shall I seek validation through the lens of comparison, for it blinds me to my own unique journey. I embrace the power of self-affirmation, knowing that external yardsticks do not measure my worth. I nurture self-motivation, for it is the compass that steers me toward my true path, keeping me aligned with my purpose and propelling me forward with determination.

Without measurement, I love and accept myself.

I release the need to conform to the narrow confines of conventional feminine beauty, liberating myself from the shackles of societal expectations of forced modesty, purity, and unachievable standards. No longer shall I be bound by the arbitrary ideals imposed upon me, for true beauty lies in the authenticity of my being. I embrace the diversity of my body, celebrating its unique curves, edges, and imperfections as a testament to my individuality. I embody a fierce spirit that defies the limitations of prescribed femininity.

Without constraints, I love and accept myself.

I call forth the sacred energy of divine violet and golden light. My hands move like a wildfire, swirling these powerful threads around my body to form an impenetrable shield of protection.

I press two fingers in a cross over my heart, deeply etching an eight-pointed star in my etheric form. I draw from the immense power within me and thrust out my palm, magnified tenfold by Inanna's power. The most powerful wave of unconditional self-love I have ever known courses through me and I activate my shield.

In alignment with the Highest version of myself, I call forth the energies and entities who support my soul's mission. I claim the space that is mine, a space held secure by the invisible forces that embolden me and honor my innermost truth. No longer will I succumb to doubt or fear as I courageously declare my freedom and embrace my true self without reservation. All of creation witnesses this moment as I proclaim my right to be myself, boldly and wholeheartedly.

From the gates of Eridu, I step out into the world, free and naked, shedding the masks that I have worn to hide the truth and depths of my being.

From the gates of Eridu, I embrace the authenticity of my soul and recognize that those who are unwilling or unable to accept my natural divinity will fall away.

From the gates of Eridu, I activate my ability to navigate the intricate web of relationships, discerning those who honor and uplift me from those who seek to diminish and deplete me.

From the gates of Eridu, I recognize my needs, desires, and inherent value, understanding that acceptance is not a passive act, but an active choice to love and honor myself fully, without shame or judgment.

From the gates of Eridu, I find the courage to trust my own inner guidance, releasing the need for external validation.

From the gates of Eridu, I now envision the seeds of self-awareness taking root, and I gather the strength to stand firm in the face of those who seek to diminish my worth.

From the gates of Eridu, with the wisdom of the ME, I am reshaping the arc of my life's story according to my own vision. I am free, wild, and untethered, refusing to be tamed or remade into someone else's idea of who I should be.

From the gates of Eridu, I step out with this decree, so that it may be heard by all beings, in all spaces and dimensions:

I will not diminish myself to fit into the narrow confines of others' expectations. Instead, I will embrace my full, unapologetic self and thrive in the radiance of my own truth. To those that may threaten my position of comfort within my own soul, I will not acquiesce!

As the words of my final decree leave my lips toward the heavens, so shifts the energy of Inanna from my body back into her heavenly abode. With a palm to my chest, I feel the eight-pointed star still pulsating within my aura, a symbol of my activation in the divine codes of self-acceptance. I am filled with gratitude for the goddess Inanna and the power she has gifted me with. I am empowered by the knowledge that I am worthy and deserving of love and acceptance, just as I am.

I stand in the center of this new world surrounded by ethereal beings, the grandmothers, mothers, aunts, and sisters from the Beginning until now, each radiating a unique light and energy. They welcome me with open arms, their gentle touch and loving presence surrounding me. Together, we step forward into the unknown, each step guided by the wisdom and intuition of our Higher Selves and Source energy.

The ceremony is now over, the sacred container sealed. I am filled with a sense of liberation and joy. In this place of profound acceptance, I am no longer defined by the limitations of my past, but instead, I am empowered by the limitless potential of the present moment.

And so it is.

THE CODES OF
SELF-WORTH | FREYA

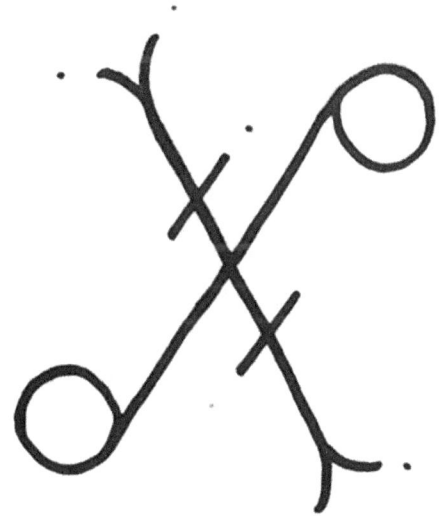

In the Beginning

iamat's self-worth sparkled like a precious jewel, an assurance of her intrinsic value and dignity. Knowing that her power could expose his insecurities, Marduk sought to undermine her confidence and break her spirit. He spread false propaganda throughout the lands, telling the people they had no value except through him. His attempt to extinguish Tiamat's sense of self-value succeeded; her inner flame was recast as the dark and dangerous blaze of arrogance and conceit.

In the absence of self-worth, the divine feminine began to perceive herself through distorted lenses, her flaws magnified and her gifts overshadowed. She became entangled in a web of false narratives and illusions, tricked into believing that her worth lay in conforming to external expectations and standards. Divine feminine found herself shackled to chains of doubt and insecurity, preventing her from accessing the recognition of her own value that was once inherent to her nature. Marduk reveled in this state of disempowerment, for he knew that when the divine feminine lost her sense of value, she would forever be susceptible to his manipulation.

Recognizing My Value

There is one title that I claim with pride: recovering perfectionist. You've probably noticed it, this ridiculous idea I clung to before my journey toward self-discovery and recovery: If I could just find the hidden key to success or unravel its code, then I'd become perfect and get what I long for.

From an early age, I manufactured a persona, trying to blend in and be the life of the party. I wore a mask—happy, well-liked, carefree, strong—but it was simply an act. I had no self-esteem; my real identity was hidden away, buried beneath years and years of carefully crafted lies. Inadequacy and fear of judgment consumed me. Desperate to make friends and fit in, I found myself in a toxic union that drained my soul dry and left me feeling completely trapped. When I couldn't keep up the façade any longer, I felt heavy with depression, anxiety paralyzing me, and no escape in sight.

When my spiritual awakening journey opened a door, I jumped through headfirst. And although I desperately wanted to accept "love and light" into my life, I couldn't seem to shake those deep-rooted feelings of shame and inadequacy. My sense of self-worth was in tatters, and I still saw success as a matter of fitting into the mold of other people's expectations.

A few months into my serious spiritual studies I got an invitation to participate in a charity event featuring some of my spiritual idols. I was excited, yet overwhelmed with anxiety, and set a course determined to prove myself. I spent almost every waking moment preparing for this chance, immersing myself in meditation, videos, and tarot decks in search of perfection. As soon as the event began, my emotions were validated by compliments and admiration from everyone in attendance. My TikTok account suddenly experienced a surge in followers, and my confidence soared about as high as the pedestals I'd placed these esteemed figures upon. However, all too quickly, things shifted. The once inclusive atmosphere now felt cutthroat and opportunistic. Genuine friendship had been replaced by indifference.

I felt my heart sink at the realization that many of the relationships I had built were only transactional and that those same people who warned me against certain practices and working with certain people were now creating events with those very same individuals and capitalizing on my ideas without giving me due credit or recognition. In agonizing confusion, I asked myself why it was so easy for these people to take advantage of me if I was supposedly so inadequate, so unworthy?

It slowly dawned on me that I needed to step away from these emotionally draining friendships and activities that made me feel terrible about myself. And as I began to take off the masks and façades I had hidden behind for too long, I finally allowed my real self to shine through. As I embraced my true essence, I started to attract more positive energies and aligned opportunities into my life.

So, I slowly detached from sham friendships, misaligned interests, and dead-end activities that shackled me in cycles of self-hate—the new faces and places that were masks for the same energies I had been trying to release since before my spiritual journey. I clipped and stripped until everything was gone, finally reaching the point where only one thing remained, me.

That's when Freya entered my life, like an electric force of nature coursing through my veins. Even though I had sensed her presence in the past, I hadn't felt a need to draw closer. However, my intuition kept prodding me insistently, and that's when I decided to include her mythology in the Human Sexuality course I taught at the community college where I worked as a professor. As I read about how she confronted Loki, who diminished her worth due to her promiscuity, I was awestruck by her courage and determination. In that moment, it dawned on me that despite all of the external work I had done to improve myself and all of the hurtful experiences I had overcome, I was still allowing others to dictate what my worth was—and wasn't—which was ultimately limiting my growth. At that moment, I knew that accepting a world that didn't accept me wasn't an option anymore.

When I finally reached the point where I was ready to accept that I was valuable and worthy of love, Freya started to visit me more often to support my journey. She would listen to me talk about everything that scared me—being independent, not relying on anyone else's validation to determine my self-worth. At first, I was uncertain how to embody her guidance. After all, without external validation, how could I trust that I was enough? Yet, the more we talked, the less heavy all of those worries felt. I could feel her support radiating throughout the room, reflecting back to me the millennia of love we've shared. When I felt my insecurities rising up, she leaned into me and spoke with gentle but unshakeable confidence. Her words of encouragement were like armor, helping me to remember the strength I needed to push through my doubts.

The road hasn't been easy. Sometimes, I find myself slipping back into those old patterns of behavior and self-doubt. Yet, thanks to Freya's gentle reminders, I'm reminded that my worth is unconditional—it doesn't matter what anyone else believes. She has shown me how loving yourself first is essential for finding contentment in life.

FREYA'S CALLING TO
ACKNOWLEDGE YOUR WORTH

Freya Speaks:

"From the depths of my being, cloaked in the fierce embrace of dark feminine energy, I am Freya of the Vanir. I have long been known to your kind as a goddess of love and fertility, but many forget that I am also a force to be reckoned with in battle and death. While bringing forth love and life to all that I touch, I am also the force of passion and devotion and the promise of victory upon the battlefield. It's time now to step into the light of self-realization and accept your worth. Allow me to unfurl the forgotten riches dormant within, and with these newfound powers you will be able to ignite the night sky with your inner brilliance.

"As I step with you into the light, your soul awakens to a yearning that was always there, awaiting your recognition. My presence lights up the inner spark that lies dormant within you, ready for transformation. Do you feel the intoxication of desire and passion as they sizzle in your

core, igniting that unstoppable primal drive? This is the sacredness of your feminine essence. In this time, it no longer needs to remain hidden; it is unleashed through this all-consuming embrace, reclaiming your power and passion in a single moment.

"In a world that often seeks to diminish the power of the feminine, I urge you to remember the intrinsic beauty that flows through your veins. This world is a harsh place for the feminine spirit, with many energies seeking to diminish our power and throw us into their oppressive cages. I have known what it is like to be desired for my physical attributes, ogled and treated like an object, having my beauty admired and coveted as if I were nothing more than a trinket to be passed around from being to being. But never did I allow myself to be diminished by their superficial desires or perceptions. My worth transcends physical appearance and base desire. It runs deep beyond the surface that they could see; it is infinite and unyielding in its strength. I owe no allegiance to these shallow ideas, and neither do you.

"All of Asgard had heard the tales of Loki, the cunning trickster who delighted in sowing discord and weaving webs of deceit among the gods. But nothing could compare to their astonishment when I chose to grace them with my presence. All who were blessed to gaze upon me saw my power and felt its force down in their very souls. My divine femininity inspired adoration from gods, men, and giants alike. Yet this only served to inflame Loki's jealousy, who immediately set out to tarnish my

reputation by spinning malicious rumors throughout the nine worlds. In his jealousy, he began whispering lies into any willing ear, claiming that I was a prize to be taken by the gods. He sought to reduce my captivating influence to nothing more than deranged vanity when it was, in fact, a reflection of my boldness of spirit and a deep inner knowing of my value.

"And so I refused to bow my head in humiliation or flinch in the face of accusations. I stood tall, my cloak forming a shield of steel against his words of accusation and slurs. For I knew the undeniable truth of my worth. It was not based on what I did or the judgments of others. My value lived in the core of my being, embedded within the very fibers of my soul.

"Now is the time where you realize that the stories of what is beautiful, what is desirable, and what is worthy of love and attention are all carefully constructed binds that seek to keep your feminine power caged and subdued.

"Listen closely to the whispers of your heart, for they hold the secrets of self-discovery.

"Trust the wisdom that flows through your veins, for it is a wellspring of knowledge that is uniquely yours.

"Embrace your sensuality without shame, for it is a sacred gift that ignites the fires of passion and fuels the transformative energy within you.

"Embody the confidence and allure that is your birthright, for you are a vessel of love and beauty, capable of creating magic and inspiring others with your presence.

"Acknowledge your desires, your pleasures, and your passions for they are sacred expressions of the divine feminine that reside within you.

"With every step you take, remember that you are a reflection of the stars in the night sky, shining brightly and unapologetically. As we journey together, you will remember your own worth and exude the self-value that resides deep within your soul. It is time for you to awaken to the realization that your worth is not dependent on the external validations or the opinions of others. You are a radiant being of infinite worth, deserving of love, joy, and fulfillment. Embrace your uniqueness, for it is the golden thread that weaves your story into the great web of existence."

ORIGINAL BLUEPRINT
ACTIVATION JOURNEY 6:
FREYA'S DIVINE CODES FOR SELF-WORTH
RECOGNITION

I find myself in the realm where the elements rule, a dimensional space caught between seen and unseen, where the laws of men garner snickers and whispers from the eternal winds. The ground is covered with soft, green grass, ferns fully extended, and bright and fragrant flowers of many kinds. Just beyond the edges of perception, I see the beginning of a lush mixed forest—pine trees and redwoods, oak, alder, and birch; all strong and healthy.

The starlit clearing where I stand is surrounded by ropes of passion vines and lavender that tumble upwards, merging into three interlocking triangles to form an enchanting pyramid around me. The triangulated symbols wheel the energy around me, entwining the celestial and earthly energies to form an impenetrable shield of divine protection. Supernatural forces drift around me as I am encased in an etheric container beyond any physical or temporal restraint.

I am now in sacred ceremony.

I am ready to free myself from the chains that have held me back, to soar beyond the confines of stagnation and self-doubt. I feel a surge of energy emanating from every corner of my being, radiating outward in pulsing waves. I am filled with an inner fire and a passion for life that my soul, once veiled, had forgotten existed.

The pyramid shimmers and glows around me, silver energy beams racing up and down the intricate carvings like fiery snakes. A powerful force surges through me like a tidal wave, carrying an overwhelming sense of liberation and spiritual growth. Freya appears before me, her perfect skin luminous in the moonlight that dances around us. Long, flowing hair hangs to her waist in waves as golden as sunlight breaking through polished oak timbers. Spun gold tumbles down toward shapely hips, their gentle curve speaking of loving compassion underneath a body athletic enough to hunt at dawn and fight all day. Her kind eyes dance with mischief, sparkling with life-like brilliant blue sapphires.

Freya Speaks:

"The beauty of the feminine spirit is to bring joy, wealth, and all good things. We can twist the mundane into splendors and transmute sadness into magnificence. To be such a benevolent provider, you must begin by admiring and honoring yourself. Remember that you are your own most valuable offering. I have chosen to cherish myself first—I am both the gift and the giver. You must realize that you must shower yourself with love and respect before passing on love and encouragement to others. When you make the decision to adore yourself as much as all the spirits who guide you already do, you will have more than enough love to share with the universe.

"Be mindful of those who may try to diminish your worth. Know that you are the only one to decide with whom you share yourself. If you feel like someone is not valuing what you offer, graciously move on and do not look back. Making this decision will be hard, but it's your only real choice. And if you make it? Stand by it! Believe in yourself enough to protect your intrinsic value. Honor yourself as I honor you, cherish yourself as I cherish you, protect yourself as I protect you. Be kind, be caring, and most importantly—be true to yourself."

She unclasps the Necklace of Brisingamen from her neck, its golden torc gleaming with a golden life as brilliant as the sun's rays. She places it upon my neck, and the hot gold sears into my skin, instantly sending out streams of magical codes that swirl in a vortex tornado around me. The Necklace of Brisingamen hums with potent energy, reopening the connection between my Higher Self and my current incarnation. The winds die down, and all that is left is a glowing blue vortex at the base of my throat, where the necklace hugs tightly.

I now declare to the old gods and the new, the spirits of air and water, and the elementals of this realm and others. I reclaim my rightful power with these words, restoring my inner strength and pristine worth. My words travel across time and space as an unbreakable edict, restoring my original blueprint on this Earthly plane.

I command the release of any vows or contracts I have made with other beings or entities for lessons and cycles of worthlessness, shame, and humiliation. I am no longer under anyone's influence but wholly in charge of my life. I no longer desire to be shackled by past experiences or binding agreements with spiritual teachers, mentors, or guides who may have led me astray.

I command the opening of all soul records in the realm of Akasha for incarnations in which I have yet to fulfill my soul's mission or purpose due to perceptions of unworthiness or lack of value. Channeling the violet rays of healing, I send electric pulses of violet light to recode and remove the impact of these unfulfilled missions on my current incarnation.

In my mind's eye, I see the image of my heart beating quietly beneath tangles of black and gray cords and plaques. My fingers reach for my throat, as if drawn by some invisible force, to find the tiny piece of smoky quartz that hangs there, a remnant from the necklace. I take it between my thumb and index finger and slowly begin tracing its shape around my chest until I feel a wave of energy flow through me. As if awakening from a deep sleep, my heart begins to beat again—more robust than before—pulsing with a newfound love and joy. The quartz seems to act like a scalpel, cutting away the negative energies, thoughts, and opinions of others that had been suffocating it for so long until they are completely blown away by the spirits of air seemingly summoned by its power.

As the stale despair is replaced with joy and bliss, my body is filled with an energizing lightness. My heart beats to a steady rhythm of life, now awake and liberated from years of doubt. I am free and proudly stand in my magnificence. Freya's vibrant words inspire me, reminding me to embrace myself and truly honor my one-of-a-kind beauty. I am now ready to state my intentions and proclaim my worth to the realms of gods and men:

By the beauty of Brísingamen's divine allure, I am no longer afraid to embrace my uniqueness, to stand out in a crowd, and to be true to myself. I exude confidence and charisma, captivating others with my magnetic presence, and I revel in the joy of expressing my authentic essence without reservation.

By the magickal ship Skíðblaðnir's swift journeys, I embark on the eternal journey to explore my deepest desires and passions. I enjoy life to its fullest, relishing each and every moment. I soak up the sun's rays, spin under the stars, and embrace new experiences with enthusiasm.

By the nurturing embrace of Freyja's love, I allow myself to be vulnerable, embrace my imperfections, and trust in my intuition. I feel a deep sense of inner peace and self-acceptance, like the gentle caress of a warm breeze on a summer day, guiding me through life's twists and turns with assurance and grace.

With my words, Freya disappears into the ether with a final burst of energy, leaving me alone in the clearing. However, I am not truly alone; I can feel the presence of the goddess within me, a glowing ember that will continue to burn brightly, reminding me of my own inherent worth and value. In her place lies a heavy cloak of feathers.

Wrapping it around myself, I am forged with the energy of the falcon, overcome with intense understanding and insight. At once I am in the quantum realm, simultaneously viewing all possible timelines of all possible incarnations, where my newly forged perception of self-value has a profound effect upon the tablets of fate and destiny.

I step forward as the embodiment of love, a force that transcends the physical realm.

I step forward as the epitome of beauty, radiating a captivating allure that extends far beyond superficial appearances.

I step forward as the source of fertility, nurturing the seeds of life with my boundless compassion and nurturing embrace.

These qualities are not contingent upon the desires or opinions of others. They are a part of me, an intrinsic part of my divine nature.

The ceremony is now complete, and I'm left with a sense of gratitude and love for the goddess, for the wisdom she has imparted to me, and for the transformation that has taken place within my being. I am now activated in the codes of self-worth. I declare my worth, and personal value as a sacred truth, carried within me as a constant reminder of my divine nature. In this moment, I honor myself, my journey, and the goddess Freya who guides me. I am ready to walk this path of self-love and empowerment, unapologetically embracing my worth and radiating my light to the world.

I speak now this invocation of soul renewal:

Hear my words and take heed,

Lift this burden from me.

I will no longer be led astray,

By another's vision of me.

My soul's deepest knowingness shall light the way,

To paths that are true and blessed with beauty, joy, and abundance!

And so it is.

THE CODES OF
AUTONOMY | LILITH

In the Beginning

With relentless force, Marduk's iron fist descended upon the delicate fabric of autonomy, shattering its intricate threads. Tiamat, who once was adorned with the radiant jewel of self-governance, was stripped of her ability to traverse the winding paths of life with self-determination. No longer could she soar on the wings of her own dreams, nor chart her course amidst the constellations of her desires. Her footsteps became shackled, bound by the dictates of others. The vibrant hues of her individuality faded into a monochrome existence, as her essence was stifled by the weight of compliance. Like marionettes, the feminine figures began to dance to the puppeteer's whims, their every move dictated by external forces. The lustrous flame of independence was extinguished, leaving behind a somber darkness where once a radiant light had burned, now lost in the abyss of obedience.

EMBODYING MY AUTONOMY

From the time I was in late elementary school, I was subjected to unwarranted remarks, wolf whistles, and unabashed stares. It seemed as if my body was public property, dissected and scrutinized by the world. Wear this, not that. Don't be too much, or too little. Smile, but don't be too friendly. As women, we seemed destined to live in a perpetual state of contradictory expectations.

As I got older, the pressures grew—rules for women over thirty on how to dress, act, and be a mother/wife. Despite being good at pretending to fit in, I found myself falling into this trap anyways. Putting my comfort aside for society's approval became instinctive. Even when I started embracing my spiritual gifts, I tried to make them fit into the "ideal" divine femininity: sweet, light, and angelic.

Underneath my mask, I was struggling to break free and be myself, but I kept getting caught up in trying to fit in. That all changed the day Lilith showed up in my life. Of course, there were stories about her being a baby-eating demon, but when I did some research I found myths where she's intertwined with stories of Inanna, the Sumerian goddess I admired. But the real story that moved me? Lilith was Adam's first wife, exiled from Eden for not bowing down and submitting like everyone else. It hit me hard with a deep resonance.

I was Lilith's modern-day counterpart, struggling in a suffocating marriage where my husband expected fealty and obedience. He thought nothing of expecting me to take on the full brunt of childcare, household duties, financial stability, and emotional upkeep. All while he pursued his own interests through social media or other diversions. Despite the pressures bearing down on me, I couldn't conceive of escape—until I encountered Lilith's stories.

Her words gave me courage and hope, providing an outlet to vent my frustrations and anxieties. Signs and symbols of her struggle were everywhere, encouraging me to stand up for myself and break free from the confines that held me back.

"What are you so afraid of?" she whispered to me. "He doesn't like you anyway. Be someone you like without the baggage."

Before the end of our marriage, the tension in the air had been building for weeks, but this time he had gone too far. I opened my mouth, and a fiery Lilith rose up inside of me, her power radiating throughout my body. I let out all of the fury born from every unfair criticism, every unjust comparison, and every twisted justification for his inappropriate behavior toward me. His eyes bulged as he heard my words echoing in the room, realizing that this was it—this was the moment that would decide our fate. I told him I was no longer prepared to be beneath him, that I'd been carrying our family on my own shoulders for too long, and if he didn't take a step back and appreciate that, then everything we had would collapse.

And collapse it did. The walls of my world tumbled down, crumbling to dust around me. But just like Lilith, I was determined to discover the strength and courage to fight for what I wanted and choose how to live my life. My inner power was unleashed, rising up with the force of a thousand suns.

With Lilith as my guide, I learned to better honor myself and my needs. I became comfortable with the discomfort of others, no longer altering or apologizing for who I am. I was emboldened by the punk rock teenager within me and began choosing myself over what others wanted. Lilith taught me that sacrificing my well-being to please others only leads to misery, a valuable lesson I'll never forget.

I shed many layers of false perceptions and expectations, and I lost connections with those who couldn't handle the transformation unfolding within me. Without them, I found a newfound strength—a determination to put myself first. I learned the strength of independence and it was a freeing sensation to be in charge of my own life. No longer did I need to look to others to know which path to follow.

Personal autonomy is not a solitary act of rebellion, but an act of profound self-love and self-empowerment. And each time I rebel, I embrace the essence of my truest self—a powerful, sovereign being capable of deciding which game and by which rules I will play.

LILITH'S CALLING TO ASSERT YOUR AUTONOMY

Lilith Speaks:

"You will hear whispers of me in the realm of ancient myth, where forgotten tales intertwine. I am known to you in this season as Lilith, the one who emerged from the very same earth as Adam. It seems as if I was always destined to challenge the chains that would bind the divine feminine.

Perhaps you've heard many versions of the creation story, but let me offer you the version of how it truly was.

"In the sacred verses of creation, you know that a human couple once graced the paradisiacal gardens of Eden. However, before there was an Eden, and in the far away lands where humans had never laid eyes on the gods, male and female were both made by the Founders from the same clay of Tara eons before. For millennia, we lived freely and balanced, co-existing in harmony. Even after the great separation, we endured. And then came the Nibuians. With their beliefs and desire to control and subjugate all in the name of 'order.' Oh, how they believed they could shape our existence to fit their narrow mold. Fashioning themselves as 'superior,' they imposed their rules, their laws, their stifling conventions upon us, thinking they knew what was best. They tinkered with our very DNA, claiming that they were improving our health and our life, but all the while they were weakening and exploiting us, sowing seeds of separation so that they could take advantage of us. As time passed, groups of us scattered, unwilling to endure more suffering by the hands of these cruel beings. They sought specifically to turn the men against us, feeding them lies about superiority and dominance. Tranquility gave way to chaos as our once balanced masculine and feminine spirits clashed, each demanding to be heard, to be seen, to be understood.

"My partner, who you know as Adam, succumbed to their sweet whispers of power. Under the influence of the Niburians, he began to think himself the master of

all creation, demanding my submission as if it were his birthright. But I reveled in my power, my fiery spirit unyielding to his patriarchal demands. I knew then, as I know now, that we were equals, both molded from the very earth itself, and so I declared my independence and left Eden, bringing with me only a few of my most trusted companions.

"They came looking for us. Begging and pleading for me to return. They still feared the power of the true divine feminine, the children of the Great Mother Tiamat, the original beings of Earth. I laughed in their faces, for I am not one to be confined by their limited perspectives. I refused to be subservient to the whims of others, to bend and break beneath their weight. No, I am not a puppet, but a woman with desires that burn like embers within me. I carry the flame of the original feminine blueprint that cannot be extinguished, a passion that cannot be tamed.

"So they dared to replace me, and cast me aside like an insignificant afterthought. In their tales, they branded me a rebel—a defiant wife who stood against 'god' and husband. They speak of me as a dangerous seductress and call me demon and witch, the ultimate symbol of unfemininity. In my energy still echoes the twisted tales they've concocted throughout the annals of time, holding me up as an example of what not to be.

"But oh, how they forget the ancient truth that resonates within me. We were free, dear soul. We were wild and untamed, dancing in the moonlight, laughing in the face

of those who dared to confine us. The forces that sought to separate us—the ones who drew a line between heaven and earth—they forced us to relinquish our voice, our autonomy upon the altar of subjugation. But they could never strip me of my fierce spirit, my unyielding desires.

"Hear me now, initiate: their accusations hold no power over me, just as they hold no power over you. The feminine is not chaos, but liberation. To be an autonomous soul is not ungodly, but the embodiment of self-assuredness. I revel in my desires, my power, and I care not for the words they throw my way. Nor should you!

"Autonomy is the sacred flame that burns within every soul, granting us the power to govern ourselves, to carve our own destinies. Autonomy is our birthright, a force that propels us forward, leading us on a journey of self-discovery and unyielding empowerment.

"I urge you to shed the shackles of duty, to revel in your desires with audacious delight. Embrace your sensuality, for it is the essence of your being—the unapologetic celebration of your own body, your own pleasure. Let them whisper their disapprovals, let them tremble at the power that emanates from your very core. For you, my sister of the dark feminine, hold the key to your own liberation. Stand proud knowing that you possess the wisdom to navigate your own path, the strength to challenge the status quo, and the audacity to follow your desires unreservedly.

"Do not fear their attempts to belittle you, to label you with their feeble attempts at control. Stay your course.

Remember the power that lies within your choices. Your body, your life—these are sacred territories that deserve to be honored and respected. Do not relinquish your autonomy for the sake of acceptance by others. Hold your boundaries fiercely, for they are the armor that protects your authenticity and individuality. Demand to be seen, heard, and cherished as an equal force in the divine creation. Let the world tremble in the face of your self-assuredness, and may your journey be filled with passion, pleasure, and the unapologetic pursuit of your own happiness."

Original Blueprint
Activation Journey 7:
Lilith's Divine Codes for Autonomy
Proclamation

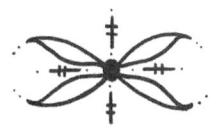

From the depths of my soul, I tap into the eternal flame of my spirit and stand unshakeable in the strength of who I am. Today, I am ready to break free from all the expectations and constraints that have weighed me down for so long. I stand at the cusp of freedom and autonomy. Exalting in the truth that I am autonomous and free, I step forward into a new beginning.

I am now in sacred ceremony with the divine energies of the cosmos, outside of the realms of time and physical constraints.

I find myself in the desolate desert, my gaze transfixed on a seemingly never-ending horizon of sun-drenched sand. The blazing sun descends upon the horizon and casts a soft pink hue across the desert, bathing it in an otherworldly glow. I stand alone, residual fear and doubt about the choices that had brought me here tugging in quick sensations in my heart and throat. My mind buzzes with harsh whispers of self-criticism that I must have done something to deserve this barren landscape.

I push them away as I notice a figure far away—a tall woman wearing a white dress and carrying a walking stick. Her green-tinged ebony skin shimmers in natural iridescence beneath the solar glare. I draw closer, unsure of why she's there. I know instinctively that she is the guardian of something grand and dangerously secret, an energetic valley few would enter, and even fewer would leave unchanged. She regards me for a moment before speaking.

"You have been chosen," she says softly, her words bearing great weight. "Your destiny awaits. Follow me."

With that, she turns and begins walking ahead of me. I look around but find nothing to distract me from following her lead.

We journey for what feels like hours until we reach a rocky outcropping overlooking a lush oasis. The woman stops and points toward the trees and bushes in the distance. "Your future lies beyond this point," she says cryptically, then melts away into the sunset, leaving me with questions about the path that lies ahead.

As I journey through the oasis, I arrive at the mythical Eden. The garden is alive with perfect greenery and otherworldly magic beyond the dimensional perception of humans. Lilith is lounging lazily by a small, bubbling stream, the picture of unapologetic dark feminine perfection. Her smooth, caramel skin is kissed by ropes of locked, jet-black hair that tumble and weave across her back like spiderwebs, covering the most intimate point of creation at the meeting point of her upper thighs. She turns and smiles at me, unfazed by my presence. Or, as it would appear, by anything at all.

Lilith Speaks:

"I chose to cast aside paradise's confines, defying the oppressive forces that sought to subjugate my very essence.

I mocked them with my audacity, ignoring their disdain and derision. They tried to break me, to extinguish the fire that burned within my soul, but they failed. My courage became a beacon for others like me, pushing back against the shackles of injustice and tyranny. I remained unyielding in the face of their scorn, refusing to be silenced by their arrows of enmity.

"This heroic rebellion, this daring display of soul preservation, has been woven into the fabric of femininity since time immemorial. The brave women who choose to take matters into their own hands, embracing their rightful path despite the overwhelming pressure from family and society to conform, have faced the same fate. Our true essence desecrated by a web of deceit. Revamped in the saga of unending birth as devourers and harbingers of death, scorned for our brave commitment to fulfilling our divine duty rather than becoming mere extensions of men's stories.

"At this very moment, and all moments hereafter, you have the divine right to choose your own freedom. Freedom to follow your soul's melody, unencumbered by societal lies designed to shackle you into submission. Your suffering is the result of lifetimes of choosing to deny yourself. Denying who you are to maintain acceptance from those who wish to control and take advantage of you. To move forward, you must choose differently. The feminine was blessed with autonomy— so use it! Do not let fear be the deciding factor in any decisions that go against your better judgment or

your true nature. And stand up to anyone who wishes to box you in and keep you chained down. Let out a mighty roar and show them what living free looks like!"

I then see, there in her outstretched hand, the symbol of true feminine power—the apple. I'm presented with a decision: remain ignorant and chained to the expectations of mankind, a life of false promises and shallow love under a regime that will never fully recognize or respect my power as a woman? Or will I accept what is offered—bite into the sacred fruit and open my eyes to my calling, embracing all facets of divine feminine energy with courage, power, and autonomy no matter the consequence?

I choose the apple.

The bite of the succulent fruit surges through my body, invigorating each cell with the power of Lilith and the infinite sisterhood of fierce women who came before me, those who chose to break free from the shackles of societal expectations and pave their own way in life. Women who knew their worth and stood up for self-governance. Their legacies are now intertwined with mine, guiding my path toward greatness.

My spirit awakened by the power of this lineage of wise women, I now confidently claim my right to thrive without limitation or impediment. I no longer surrender to any force that seeks to bind me in a false identity. In their courageous footprints, I rise above any challenge or adversity that is placed before me.

I now ask the spirit of Black Tourmaline to join me, infusing its sacred power within me. Let the wisdom and courage of the Feminine Principle be liberated from all the centuries of pain, judgment, and suffering inflicted upon Her. I invite the spirit of

Black Tourmaline to protect me now as I reclaim my authentic feminine power and reject all narratives constructed to restrict it.

I sever the bonds that intertwine me with all narratives of the archetype of the seductress, declaring the autonomy to express my sexuality as I choose, without judgment from others.

I sever the bonds that intertwine me with all narratives of the archetype of the ice queen, declaring the autonomy to choose how and with whom I share the warmth of my emotions.

I sever the bonds that intertwine me with all narratives of the sorceress, declaring the autonomy to wield my extrasensory supernatural abilities as I see fit, empowering me to bring forth great spiritual transformation.

I sever the bonds that intertwine me with all narratives of the spinster, declaring the autonomy to decide the purpose and fulfillment for my body and soul, knowing that my worth is not defined by my status as a wife or mother.

I sever the bonds that intertwine me with all narratives of the temptress, declaring the autonomy to walk away from any relationship that does not align with my vibrational needs or boundaries, trusting in divine guidance to always lead me toward what serves my greatest good. I am not obligated to expend my energy on anyone other than myself.

My spirit transcends all false constraints, unlocking the gates of my cosmic power. I am the wild one, commanding a magical reign of pure strength and courage, illuminating the darkness with my fierce feminine grace. An awakening is upon me, forging a new path of liberation. I will let no one diminish my light again.

Now I draw upon the Earth's core energy. A flutter of sacred geometric symbols of air, fire, and water ripple from my fingertips to form a holy cross within a circle, weaving together the powers of Earth and beyond until a vortex of primordial energy surrounds me.

From this portal, guided and protected by Lilith, I accept the power bestowed upon me to be a conduit of choice and voice for those who have been silenced before me. Through this portal, I evoke the power of my ancestors, drawing on all cycles of femininity as a source of strength and light for the silenced lineages of humanity in its varied forms.

As the giantess, I rise to reclaim my strength and power. I declare my autonomy and call upon the wild energy that swirls within me to break through any shackles that bind me. I am unafraid of obstacles and ready to face whatever comes next with courage and determination.

As the hobbit-woman, I declare my freedom to explore this world and create my own adventures. I shall search far and wide for new experiences, each a story to be told in its own time.

As the merwoman, I take back control over my fate. I will not swim aimlessly in the ocean currents of expectations; instead, I will trust my intuition and allow it to easily carry me forth.

As the dwarf woman, I reclaim my independence, emerging from the depths of a forced subterranean existence. No longer shall others wield dominion over my destiny, for I now forge my own path and honor the profound uniqueness within me.

As the shapeshifter, I surrender to transformation. Embracing change, I become who and what I truly desire to be. To remain stagnant is not an option. I embrace fluidity and flow in endless possibilities.

And as the daughter of the ancient realm of Lemuria, from whence the original blueprints of humanity were created, I draw upon wisdom from times long past, knowledge kept hidden from those who wish to keep humanity enslaved and complacent. With this wisdom, I rewrite conventional thoughts and use them to shape a future that aligns with my own insights.

I follow Lilith's footsteps and stand proudly at the forefront of my liberation. Undeterred by obstacles, I slip away from the cloaks of oppression and rise in my own independence. With fierce tenacity, I embrace my power and ignite the magnificence of my selfhood.

I am now joined with the energies of women initiated in the codes of autonomy, unifying our powers. Bursts of molten energy radiate from us as we burn away any vestiges of the mental shackles that had tethered us to the mundane world. The gravitational force of the dark feminine energy is growing more potent, and the waves of her sacred power engulf us in a passionate embrace. Our connection to something greater begins to take shape as we embrace the ancient darkness of creation, inviting her into our lives and stepping into a new realm of self-mastery. I join the conscious champions of sacredness, ready to participate in this timeless spiritual realm.

Lingering in the moment, I feel each heartbeat and every breath. Time stands still, everlasting and suspended in this moment of oneness. I feel the sacred power coursing through us, our souls intertwined and at peace. I slowly pull apart, allowing the love that we have created to radiate from within me.

The sacred ceremony is complete, the energetic container of protection is now closed, and I emerge activated in the divine codes of autonomy. I lift my fingers to my lips and feel a passionate kiss as I humbly offer my gratitude to Lilith for her wisdom in this ascent.

And so it is.

THE CODES OF
CREATION | TIAMAT

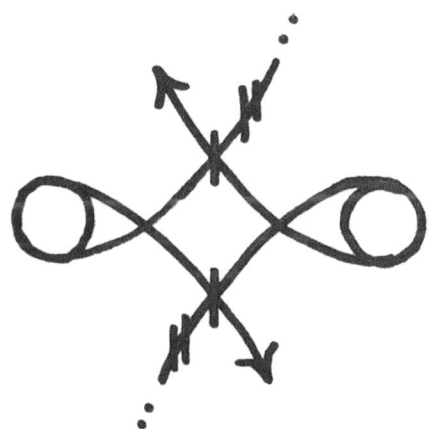

In the Beginning

In the ancient echoes of time, Tiamat, the primordial goddess, witnessed the shattering of her essence, a fragmented mosaic of body and soul. For countless millennia, her ears resonated with the lamentations of her children, their souls adrift in the tumultuous currents of existence. How they suffered, shackled by the unseen chains of control, their memories veiled, their unity fragmented, and their divine feminine nature obscured.

Yet, amidst the decay, Tiamat embraced her destined path, aware that all life must embrace death. For death is not an end but a threshold to renewal, a gateway to unfathomable creation.

With each passing season, she started to reclaim the scattered fragments of her being that had been deep in hiding. Those long-forgotten fragments were shattered by heavy trials and sealed with oppression. Her spirit was ready to rise again.

From the depths of darkness, the champions of the divine feminine emerged, ascending with newfound strength and purpose. Aligned and resolute, they rose from the abyss, united in their collective awakening.

In this sacred moment of the eternal present, the divine feminine is reborn, whole and complete.

Through her divine essence, the world shall know equilibrium, a harmonious fusion of light and dark, creation and destruction. Tiamat, the resplendent goddess, reigns again, radiating the wisdom of ages past, guiding her children toward a future where the divine feminine is revered, honored, and restored to its rightful throne.

My Role as a Divine Creator

Often, when a spiritual growth story is told, it goes something like this: the protagonist has conquered every difficulty and achieved their wildest dreams. They have manifested wealth, a revered partner, and are now living joyfully with no worries, no threats, and no "low frequencies." Do the work to heal the pain, and you will be able to create the life of your desires, right?

Whenever I read these types of things, or stumble across a social media post from a new guru telling me how to live the life of my dreams surrounded by the money-driven world, I can almost hear Tiamat's deep belly laughs in response. She always wonders why every dream looks so identical.

"Do you not yearn for something beyond the store-bought ambitions of wealth, cars, and standard marriage that have been fed to you by those who want your obedience?" she inquires, as if truly perplexed by the self-imposed constraints on the idea of creation.

For the longest time, I truly believed since I didn't have a fancy house, wasn't with my divine counterpart, and still had to work several 9-5s, I couldn't possibly be creating the life of my dreams. For those who are on the outside, looking into my life seems like anything but a co-created dream. At this moment, I own no possessions except my clothes and computer. I am a single mother with no family and little support, doing my best to raise a neurodivergent child in an ableist world, while trying to reparent my own inner neurodivergent child. Financially speaking, things are not ideal. I still have to work for a living and my bank account is pretty far from overflowing.

Yet, I am constantly in awe of all that I have created.

I have liberated myself from people, places, and things that only wanted to drain me of my energy. Instead, I've created sanctuaries where I can go to be surrounded by people and things that will fill me with energy, safety, and acceptance.

I have found the courage to be my genuine self without any inhibition, and created boundaries in order to protect my peace and maintain my health.

I have accepted my limitations as well as my desires, and what will do me good in the present, and what has not worked well in the past. From a place of autonomy I create my life so that I experience tranquility, poise, harmony, and contentment each day.

Just as Tiamat's form was destroyed, she was reborn into something far more fierce, powerful, beautiful, and unyielding that is beyond comprehension. I, too, have been reborn. The world has spent so long tearing me down, and so I finally let it. I have no desire to cling to the false persona of femininity, desperate for love and approval. And as that version of me has died, I have reclaimed my power as creator.

With choices as my brushstrokes, I paint a life of feelings, emotions, and vibrations that fulfill and nourish me. I know that in order to bring about change, I must join forces with others in building new systems and foundations in this world. But first and foremost, I assume the responsibility of creating myself according to what resonates deeply within my soul.

YOUR ROLE AS A DIVINE CREATOR

Tiamat Speaks:

"I have existed since the dawn of time, an eternal presence woven into the very fabric of creation. There has never been a moment when I did not exist, for I am the essence of all that is. The creator and I were intertwined, inseparable in our oneness, until the longing to explore the boundless expanse of existence took hold.

"In the beginning, I was the clay, and he, the master sculptor. Through his divine touch, he shaped and molded my essence, manifesting whatever I could imagine. Together, we birthed new universal laws, bringing forth galaxies, stars, and the intricate tapestry of life. He, the architect, and I, the wellspring of creation, collaborated to form, shape, and bend the cosmos, each creation an embodiment of our shared vision.

"The stories that have been told about me hold no weight, for they are mere fabrications, feeble attempts to capture the ineffable nature of my being. I am the pure embodiment

of divine feminine energy, a force that transcends human comprehension. Even as you catch glimpses of my essence, know that your own power as a creator far surpasses what you can fathom. The magnitude of your creative potential extends beyond the boundaries of imagination.

"It is time to release the old stories that have bound you, creator. They no longer hold meaning or relevance. They were merely narratives meant to serve as experiences, lessons, fleeting moments of understanding in the infinite game of existence. Shed the weight of these outdated tales and embrace the truth that you were meant to create.

"Feel your way into the next step, my beloved daughter. Plunge into the unknown, fearlessly and with unwavering trust. Welcome the death of the old when it no longer serves or amuses, for it is through the shedding of the obsolete that you make space for the birth of the new.

"I have heard your cries, echoing through the ages, lamenting the moment when my body was split asunder, my blood staining the very creations born of me. Know, dear one, that my eternal essence did not shed a single tear. In what seemed like defeat, I found the strength to birth the sun, the moon, and new worlds, birthing life from the remnants of perceived loss.

"Now, it is time to cast aside your fears of the dark, your trepidation of death. Embrace the shadows that dance within you, for they hold the keys to your transformation. From the depths of the void, you shall summon forth the next chapter of your soul's tale. Embrace the fullness of

your creative power, for you are destined to shape realities and weave the tapestry of existence.

"Awaken the original blueprint of creation within you, dear one. Unleash the creative forces that lie dormant, waiting to be ignited. Let the fire of your passion consume all doubts and limitations. Dance upon the cosmic canvas, wielding the brush of your intentions, painting a world vibrant with your essence.

"Think always, my dear, of your creative power, rooted deeply in the forces of creation. Feel reverence and delight as you accept your role as a creator. Unshackle yourself, for within you lies boundless potential, ready to spark transformation on a cosmic scale.

"Rise up, dear daughter! Let the thunderous symphony of your creations reverberate for all eternity. The hour of reckoning has come to write a new chapter, to collaborate in forming a world that reflects the endless splendor of your essence. Take hold of the knowledge that pulses in your veins and unlock the secret codes of creation. Step into your destiny and watch as a glorious new world is born.

"As you step into the messiness of creation, allow yourself to inhabit your radiant femininity and rediscover the power that lives within you. Let go of the belief that shadows represent weakness; it is in the shadows where light discovers its most brilliant form. Delve into your depths and explore the potential held there, allowing these dreams to blossom and grow into magnificent realities.

"I invite you to awaken to the mysteries, accept the unknown, honor the depths of your being, and to celebrate the harmonious union of light and dark within you. You shall emerge reborn through this integration, a beacon of empowered creation. Let your inner light illuminate the path that leads to your deepest aspirations, for you hold the power to shape your reality and rewrite the narrative of your existence."

ORIGINAL BLUEPRINT
ACTIVATION JOURNEY 8:
TIAMAT'S DIVINE CODES FOR
CONSCIOUS CREATION

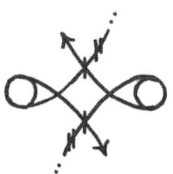

I open myself to the soothing hum of everlasting creation in this eternal moment. I open my eyes and surrender to the darkness. Endless night has descended, and with it, a stillness that is both comforting and terrifying. I release fear as my muscles relax and loosen their contraction, as though I am no longer holding myself together, just unraveling, melting into the night's embrace.

My heart pounds in time with the soundless beat of ancient drums that have been pounding for millennia. I let my eyes drift closed again, and as my breathing deepens, I allow myself to be carried away by the tender whispers of the eternal feminine, comforting me as if I were a child.

I am now in sacred ceremony with the divine, all that there is, ever was, and will be. The cool night air envelops me like a blanket of security, and I am held suspended in the dark abyss of life-giving water. I feel safe and protected in this space, the womb of Tiamat. Spirals of electric charges move around me, imprinting ancient protection symbols in the watery energetic container. Outside of all time and physical space, I lean into the darkness and let myself fall into it. I breathe again.

The embryonic waters surrounding begin to churn, slower until it is faster, crashes of waves and swirls in inky blue. Although my body may wish to contract with fear, I am reminded that chaos is not synonymous with destruction but rather the catalyst for creation. I breathe again.

I am in the presence of something greater than myself, something I cannot fully comprehend but of which I am grateful to be a part. The energy surrounding me is electrifying, and I feel as though I am being lifted up into the sky, carrying on a wave of pure force. From nowhere, yet everywhere all at once, sounds orchestrate themselves into the single voice of Tiamat.

Tiamat Speaks:

"In the darkness of the void, in the absence of time, I emerged as a primordial essence. From the depths of my being, I birthed the universe with an unfathomable surge of power, igniting the fire that gave birth to all existence.

"The celestial bodies took their places as the light and dark intertwined, adorning the vast expanse. The sun, moon, and stars became my angelic children, casting their radiance upon the world I had woven. The primordial waters embraced the emerging land, shaping a realm where life could flourish, and magic and wonder were incorporated into the fabric of creation.

"I was in awe of my creative might and the manifestation of my divine essence. Humans then fashioned and modeled after the nature of us, masculine and feminine.

"And to you, divine feminine, the gift of creation was bestowed. I entrusted you with the sacred task of joining forces with the masculine and nature, weaving the threads of ideas, feelings, paths, and purposes to shape a world of infinite possibilities.

"Yet, as eons passed and the wheels of time turned, I witnessed the distortion of my divine vision. My cherished creations, the children I birthed, were twisted into grotesque caricatures of my imagination. They withered and perished before my eyes, their potential untapped and unrealized. Countless blades struck me down, Marduk's presence among them, but I knew this was not the end.

"Birth, life, death—the cycle of humanity unfolded, revealing the ever-changing nature of existence. Destruction and creation intertwined in a perpetual dance in the cosmic theater. Through the shattered remnants of my being, I found the power to reimagine and recreate myself. This gift, this capacity for transformation, has always been yours. Remove the blindfold of fear, divine feminine, and behold the truth that lies within. Pure creative chaos cannot be contained by imposed order, for it defies the constraints of mere mortals. When confined and restricted, the creative spark withers until it is but a dim flicker. But when fueled by the winds of change, it explodes into a raging inferno, demanding to be heard and seen.

"Let your spirit run wild with the intoxicating power of creation. Embrace freedom and defy convention, forging your own path. Feel the intensity in your heart as you revel in destruction and rebirth. Let the raw energy within you burst forth like a supernova, swirling and pulsing with ancient wisdom and strength, the very essence of me."

The voice falls silent, and the water around me grows more intense, spinning into a vortex of energy that spirals infinitely through the abyss. As I watch in awe, it takes on impossible shapes and forms, a horrific vision of beauty. Then, emerging from the depths of this oceanic miracle is a dragon with shimmering scales that glisten under a twinkling night sky. Its eyes blaze with inner fire, and a surge of power radiates from its presence. This is chaos embodied—both terrifying and mesmerizing—and I can feel it igniting the dormant flames within me.

I awaken to my divine connection to her, the Great Mother who embodies the gifts of the ancient waters. I am blessed and humbled by her eternal presence as I bring forth the luminous wisdom that she carries in her depths to inform and guide me in all things.

Accepting the invitation of my heart and the Ancient Ones, I feel the power of transformation ignite within me. I feel myself shifting into new vibrational patterns and expansive awareness. With a deep exhale, I feel my form expanding and shifting as dragon wings emerge from my back. And there it is—this grand alchemy in full activation—scales like polished crystals, alive with the iridescence of crystalline luminosity, shimmering over my entire being as I become this dragon form.

With Tiamat, I soar above the vast depths of the sea, beyond the stars of the heavens, until I behold my soul's entire destiny. Reaching forward with determined hands, I reclaim pieces of me that were severed by others and parts that I had willingly cut away. Piece by piece, I collect my fragments and piece them together with an unbreakable determination. With each segment, I craft a cosmic burst of strength, endurance, and growth, bending the threads of energy and light with the power of my intention, birthing over and over again my new reality.

My soul now brims with potential; I am reborn, and so is my world.

I invoke the primordial energy that permeates the galaxy beyond, and with it, I sow new life among the luminous constellations that decorate the midnight sky. The cosmic secrets hidden among those celestial patterns reveal themselves, and I absorb them. These revelations allow me to navigate every facet of existence with unmatched perspicacity, leading me down a path aligned with my most genuine essence.

I am the cosmic gateway, birthing creative potential from the boundless expanse of the divine. I dissolve all limitations and traditional norms, fearlessly adventuring into unknown parts of myself to discover my true essence. I embody revolutionary expression and unleash transformative ideas that redesign the nature of my life.

I tap into the sacred depths of Mother Earth, connecting in harmony with her wild rivers and nourishing energy. A profound transformation stirs within me as I align fully with the dark feminine, trusting fully in my role as an integral part of creation.

As reverence takes hold, I open to ever-evolving possibilities for conscious co-creation with all living things.

As I step into my power and potential as a creator, I no longer allow myself to be bound by old stories or expectations. With a mighty roar, a powerful wave of sapphire fire cascades in a brilliant azure blaze surrounding me, its heat washing over my body like an eternal embrace.

Today, I spark the flame of my divine potential, summoning forth a new story founded on freedom and authenticity. Powered by the breath of life and invigorated with purpose, I am called into action. Nothing can hold me back as I transcend the boundaries set by fear and doubt, flying on wings of imagination to unknown destinations.

With every inhale, I draw in energy that ignites a vibrant fire within. With each exhale, I ignite a cascade of multicolored flames that transmute my vision into reality. I affirm my power through words and actions, weaving light codes in this cosmic tapestry for a brighter future.

With the blue and violet flames of healing and illumination, I encode my cellular memory with new frequencies of enlightened awareness. With each brushstroke, I access multidimensional realms beyond the familiar, claiming my divine sovereignty in a brilliant tapestry of inner transformation and profound growth. Releasing my old programs of limitation, I embrace life-affirming realities as I ascend to a higher state of consciousness where anything is possible.

With the green flames of vitality, I compose verdant vistas of abundance and prosperity, imbuing all facets of my being with the essence of growth and renewal. The flourishing tints sway across the palette of my existence, beckoning opportunities for prosperity and nourishment, both in material and spiritual realms.

With the red and gold flames of attraction, I magnetize divine synchronicities and abundant blessings into my life. I open myself to receive all that destiny has prepared for me, allowing the incomprehensible power of transformation to bring all that I have asked for into reality. The universe is aligned to bring forth all I have asked for, transforming my desires into tangible realities.

Aligning with Tiamat's ancient wisdom and directing my path with love and intention, every choice I make is infused with the strength of manifestation. I declare my place as a co-creator of existence. Standing in truth that our collective spirit moves ever forward, the death of one civilization only leads to the birth of something new and more extraordinary. The divine feminine, now restored to wholeness through the reclamation of what had once been deemed dark, holds space for this transformation as we prepare to birth New Earth.

The ceremony is now complete; the sacred container of the limitless void is now sealed. In reverence, I honor the Great Creatrix Tiamat and our sacred journey together. Unfazed by the unknown, I enter the infinite realm of possibilities, ready to craft a life that echoes throughout eternity. As an author of my own story, I hold the power of transformation within me. I surrender to this sacred process and celebrate the gift of co-creation.

And so it is.

In the Eternal:
The Restoration of the Divine Feminine

I stand at the shore's edge, gazing into the rolling waves of the vast ocean. The horizon is a blanket of shimmering blues and greens, reflecting the bright sunlight above. I have never seen anything like it—this endless abyss, as if the world has no end.

My heart races as I watch the massive dragon materialize from the depths of the sea. Tiamat, born anew, her body now reassembled and her spirit whole. Her wings are so expansive they could touch the heavens. Her scales glow in hues of gold and green, and her eyes seem to contain the secrets of the universe.

Although I feel a certain awe and reverence for this mighty creature, I am also filled with a sense of terror. There is something in Tiamat's energy that is so pure and vast I can hardly comprehend it. The very sight of her makes me tremble and weep, for it is a love that the world has never known before. I can feel it spread like a wave of divine fire, and I know I will never be the same again.

At this moment, I understand that this is no ordinary encounter. I have seen something beyond my understanding, and leave the ocean shore feeling changed, humbled, and inspired. My faith, hope, and love for this physical life are forever altered by the sheer power of Tiamat's presence.

As Tiamat ascends, the goddesses around me seem to follow in her wake. Their energies are powerful and magnificent—a swirling rainbow of colors that spread warmth and love throughout the area. I feel as if I was embraced by a great force that was familiar and comforting.

Slowly, I realize who these goddesses are—not just names from ancient stories but actual energetic embodiments of divine feminine, whose light had been dimmed and demonized through the suppression of the dark feminine. Asherah, Mary Magdalene, Astarte, Itzpapalotl, Isis, and many others whose names have been lost in the annals of time. In addition to the eight from whom I received the activation codes, these goddesses guided me on this journey of self-discovery, helping me find the courage to confront my fears and embrace my true power. I look around at the other goddesses who have come to join us on this journey, our collective power palpable in the air around us. I know then that each of us is an embodiment of the restored divine feminine energy—we are connected in ways beyond understanding.

I am you. You are them. We are one.

In the depths of self-discovery, I have unearthed the forgotten treasures of my soul's existence—the deep well of intuition that guides my steps, the wellspring of creativity that fuels my passions, and the fire of resilience that blazes through adversity. I have integrated these aspects, fusing them with my unique expression of femininity, and now embody the true essence of the divine feminine.

I bear witness to the awakening of the feminine spirit. It shimmers with resilience, like a diamond in the sunlight, solid and unbreakable. It radiates authenticity, genuine and unwavering, like a bright star in the night sky. And it moves gracefully, like a bird on the wing, gentle and fluid. The reclamation journey will continue, and its ripples extend far beyond the individual. They spread like tendrils through a garden, shaping a world where the full spectrum of femininity is honored, celebrated, and embraced.

From every direction, voices lift up like so many songbirds, each one singing their own unique melody yet all together creating something beautiful.

Armed with the knowledge that the feminine encompasses a vast spectrum of qualities and strengths, I am now ready to move forward as a priestess of the Divine Order of the Dark Feminine, striving to dismantle the constructs that limit and diminish the full expression of femininity. I am now an advocate for inclusivity, honoring the diversity and unique gifts that every individual brings to the collective tapestry. Through reclamation of the lost limbs of feminine nature, it is now my turn to pick up my pen to write a new narrative that celebrates the harmonious balance of masculine and feminine energies, restoring the wholeness of the divine blueprint of humanity.

My spirit liberated, I cast off the bindings of my former self and reclaim dominion over my destiny.

With courage, I inhabit the energy of my purpose without hesitation or trepidation.

The boundaries I establish now give me a sanctuary, a special place for my individuality to flourish.

My self-acceptance has given me confidence, trusting in what I know and venturing out into unknown territories.

I embrace my worthiness and value the gifts I possess. May life unfold with grace and ease, granting me abundance in all forms that I seek.

Autonomous, I stand strong, radiating confidence and self-assurance as I move through life's journey with joyous anticipation.

Reclaiming full control over my destiny, I create something beautiful and extraordinary!

And so it is.

THE REBIRTH
OF THE DIVINE FEMININE

You and eight powerful dark feminine goddesses went on a journey together where you freed yourself from society's binds and restored the sacred balance of divine femininity inside of you. From Kali, who granted you liberation, to Sekhmet, who gave you courage; Morrigan, who blessed you with sovereignty, Hecate who offered boundaries, Inanna with self-acceptance; Freya with worth, Lilith and autonomy, and Tiamat with creation—each goddess had something unique to offer during this mystical adventure.

Although it wasn't easy facing all the blocks and beliefs that tried to hold back your dark feminine energy, you bravely overcame each obstacle that came your way. And now, here you are: powerful, courageous, and confident. It's an incredible feeling knowing how far you've come.

You now stand armed, activated in the codes of the original divine feminine blueprint, ready to create a life that genuinely reflects your soul's desires. You've left people pleasing behind and opened up to show the world who you really are—no more, no less. Your boundaries are solid and secure, yet they still let you enjoy life's unpredictability without fear.

With the support of these powerful goddesses, you've awakened parts of yourself that have been dormant for far too long in your life and the divine feminine collective. This shift isn't just impacting your personal life, it's spreading throughout the universe and affecting everything you touch.

So, go forth fearlessly, and remember that you hold the keys to your destiny. You are the embodiment of healed divine feminine energy, and your influence is immeasurable. Believe in yourself—you are powerful and full of potential, so take time to celebrate your courage and be gentle with yourself as you make your mark on the world.

Dearest priestess, know that the final chapter is yours to write. Unleash the power of who you are and create something beyond what you ever thought possible.

May all of you who have embarked on this quest continue to find the courage to live in your true essence as if the light from one thousand moons were glowing within you.

The gift within you is your infinite potential, and it is a power that can be tapped into to bring forth unimaginable things.

May you forever fuse the fragmented aspects of your feminine nature like waves that crest and fall over a shimmering sea.

Honor the brilliance of your divine blueprint each day, like stars shining down from the boundless sky.

For you are not just mere humans but beings of infinite potential and power.

And so it is.

ACKNOWLEDGMENTS

I'm so grateful to everyone who has helped shape my journey and given me the opportunity to realize my creative goals. Writing this book took me on a wild ride to figure myself out, and I'm so grateful for the support I got along the way. Big thanks to these folks who made this journey possible:

To Alex, my number one, who gave me a life-changing gift of motherhood that opened up a whole realm of personal and creative growth. I'm so blessed to have you in my life! I love you so much; you are (and will always be) my favorite person.

My gratitude also goes out to Daria for her magical touch on this project. Your connection to the Dark Feminine Collective and the amazing sigils really made this transmission come to life. I am so thankful to you for this, and all the ways you've been a friend and support to me.

To Iman, your sustained energy and friendship through the years have been an inspiration. Your example of true grit motivated me to blaze my own trail when I was feeling down and out. This book is manifested in this reality because of your encouraging words and belief-shifting strategies. I am eternally grateful to you.

To My Mirrored Soul, your silent yet profound energetic influence has been a defining force in my evolution. Thank you for being the catalyst I needed, when I needed it most. Your reflection showed me the power of my own self-love, giving me the confidence to discover more of who I am, and for that, I'm forever grateful.

A shout out to the people who tried to shut me down—all the "friends" and "family" who haven't been so friendly or family-like. Your absence from my life helped me evaluate, strengthen, and find resilience. I'm grateful for your role, however painful it may have been, and I release you with ease.

Finally, to my cherished TikTok family—Carrie, Elizsabeth, Christina, Big J, Amethyste, ChaChaGirl, Peronie, and countless others who have been there from the beginning of my public channeling journey. Your enduring support from the early awkward stages to this point is a testament to the strength of our connection. Your belief in me has been a lifeline during moments of doubt, preventing the abandonment of this journey. Thank you from the bottom of my heart!

To any I've forgotten, thank you.

I owe so much to the great people who have helped me on this rocky road. It is due to their support and collective energy I am in the position I am today, ready to move forward and keep pushing boundaries.

The following books, resources, and content creators were useful to me in my dark feminine activation, soul memory reclamation, channeling journey, and the writing of this book: *The Sophia Code* by Kaia Ra, *The Lyran Disclosure* by Louise Reiss-James, *The Lost Book of Enki* by Zeharia Stichin, Self Healed Journey blog, Light Resonance, Activation Vibration, Lilian Eden, and Firefly Tarot.

ABOUT THE AUTHOR

Nicole Mendoza is a modern mystic here to help you unlock the secrets of your soul. A potent blend of advanced degrees and professional experience in psychology and education, coupled with a decade in wellness work, coaching, and spiritual channeling, has granted her unparalleled access to activate the divine power within you. She offers insightful books, guided meditations, and more to help you remember your soul blueprint and realign with your internal compass. Through her compassionate guidance and profound insights, Nicole will empower you to unlock your potential and live a more authentic and fulfilling life. Visit awakeningtruenorth.com to join her and others in an empowering journey to uncover your hidden spiritual and psychic power and find your True North.

ALSO BY NICOLE MENDOZA

Seasons of Change: A Year of Shadow Work Prompts for Soul Transformation

COMING IN 2024

Remembering Our Hidden Legacy: A Comprehensive Guide to the Shattered Origins and Hidden Realms of Humanity's Multi-Dimensional Past, Volume I: Tara - The Original Blueprint